DEVELOPING A PERSONNEL MANUAL

DEVELOPING A PERSONNEL MANUAL
A step-by-step approach for your company

Lin Grensing-Pophal

15C978689

Self-Counsel Press
(a division of)
International Self-Counsel Press Ltd.

CENTENNIAL COLLEGE
RESOURCE CENTRE

Copyright ©1993 by International Self-Counsel Press Ltd.
All rights reserved.
No part of this book may be reproduced or transmitted in any form by any means — *graphic, electronic, or mechanical* — without permission from the publisher, except by a reviewer who may quote brief passages in a review.

Printed in Canada

First edition: May, 1993

Canadian Cataloguing in Publication Data
   Grensing-Pophal, Lin, 1959-
   Developing a personnel manual
   (Self-counsel business series)
   ISBN 0-88908-282-0
   1. Personnel management — Handbooks, manuals, etc. I. Title. II. Series.
HF5549.G73 1993   658.3   C93-091340-X

Self-Counsel Press
(a division of)
International Self-Counsel Press Ltd.

1481 Charlotte Road   1704 N. State Street
North Vancouver, British Columbia   Bellingham, Washington
V7J 1H1   98225

CONTENTS

INTRODUCTION		xi
PART I: GETTING STARTED		1
1	**WHO NEEDS A PERSONNEL MANUAL, ANYWAY?**	2
	a. What is a personnel manual?	2
	b. Why does my company need a personnel manual?	3
2	**WE'RE ALL IN THIS TOGETHER: CREATING AND WORKING WITH A TEAM**	5
	a. Forming a committee	5
	1. Formulate the purpose of the group	5
	2. Announce the opportunity to serve on the committee	5
	3. Select participants	6
	4. Schedule an initial meeting	6
	b. Working together as a team	6
	1. What is a team?	6
	2. Setting goals	7
	c. Meaningful meetings	7
	1. The agenda	7
	2. Keeping minutes	8
	3. Negotiating	9
	4. Dealing with defensiveness	10
PART II: CONSIDERING YOUR CONTENTS		13
3	**CREATING AN OUTLINE**	14
	a. What do I need to include?	14
	b. Gathering information	15
4	**THE COMPANY**	17
	a. The mission statement	17
	b. Corporate philosophy	18
	c. The organizational chart	18
	d. Job descriptions	20
	e. Who is not covered by labor standards law?	22
	1. Exempt vs. nonexempt employees — U.S. law	22
	2. Labor standards legislation — Canadian law	23
	f. Employment status	24
	1. Defining employment status	24
	2. Changes in employment status	25

5	**EMPLOYEE EVALUATIONS**	27
6	**ISSUES OF MONEY AND HOURS OF WORK**	33
	a. The nitty-gritty pay issues	33
	1. How often am I paid?	33
	2. What about overtime?	33
	3. Do I get paid more for working on holidays?	33
	4. Do I need approval for overtime?	33
	5. How do I keep track of the time I work?	33
	6. When am I paid?	34
	7. When I leave employment with unused vacation or leave, do I receive pay in lieu of time off?	34
	b. Comparable worth and pay equity	34
	c. Salary reviews	34
	d. Expenses	34
	e. Use of personal automobiles — mileage per diem	35
	f. Work hours	35
	g. Breaks	35
	h. Absenteeism	37
7	**HIRING AND FIRING**	39
	a. Promoting from within	39
	b. Hiring relatives	44
	c. Reduction in staff	44
	d. Voluntary terminations	45
	e. Involuntary terminations	46
	f. Exit interviews	46
	g. References	46
8	**BENEFITS**	48
	a. Flexible benefit programs	48
	b. Vacation	49
	c. Holidays	51
	d. Sick leave	52
	e. Personal leave	52
	f. Parental/medical leave	52
	g. Other time off	53
	1. Jury duty	53
	2. Military leave	53
	3. Funeral leave	54
	4. Doctor and dental appointments	54
	5. Elections	54
	6. General leaves of absence	54

	h.	Affect of leaves of absence on benefits	54
	i.	Insurance	55
		1. Health insurance "buy back"	55
		2. Disability coverage	56
		3. Extended benefits after leaving company	57
	j.	Sharing of company profits	58
	k.	Worker's compensation	59
	l.	Unemployment compensation	59
	m.	Employee education	59
	n.	Employee-assistance programs	60

9 GENERAL RULES AND POLICIES — 66

- a. Rules and regulations — 66
    1. Personnel records — 67
    2. Telephone procedures — 67
    3. Business gifts — 68
    4. Personal property — 68
    5. Company property — 68
    6. Contributions for gifts — 68
    7. Other contributions — 68
    8. Personal mail — 68
    9. Automobile liability coverage — 68
    10. Traffic tickets and parking violations — 69
    11. Alcohol and driving — 69
- b. Smoking/chewing tobacco — 69
- c. Drug/alcohol abuse — 70
- d. Outside employment (moonlighting) — 72
- e. Confidential nature of business — 72
- f. Sexual harassment — 73
- g. Infectious diseases — 73
- h. Problem resolution — 74
- i. Disciplinary procedures — 75
- j. Cover your bases — 76

10 LEGAL CONSIDERATIONS — 77

- a. Watch your language — 77
    1. Promises, promises... — 78
    2. Revise regularly — 78
    3. Don't limit yourself — 78
    4. Subject to change... — 79
- b. The handbook as a contractual document — 79
- c. The legal review — 81

PART III: PRESENTING YOUR INFORMATION — 83

11 DESIGN AND LAYOUT — 84
a. Format — 84
1. Perfect-bound — 84
2. Three-ring binder — 84
3. Focus on your company's needs — 85
b. Size — 85
c. Page numbering — 85
d. Finding and working with outside design help — 86
1. Choosing a designer — 86
2. Making the most of freelance talent — 86
e. Design considerations — 87
f. Finding and working with a printer — 88
g. The computerized handbook — 88
1. Gather information up front — 88
2. Garbage in — garbage out! — 88
3. Provide adequate documentation — 89

12 ORGANIZATIONAL STRATEGIES — 92
a. Table of contents — 92
b. Index — 92
c. Information at a glance — 92
d. Question and answer sections — 92
e. Phone listings — 92
f. Maps — 93
g. Conclusion — 93

PART IV: LIVING BY THE BOOK — HANDBOOK ADMINISTRATION — 101

13 DON'T STOP NOW... — 102
a. Meetings — 102
b. Bulletin board — 103
c. Suggestion box — 103
d. Testing — 103
e. Making your manual user friendly — 103

SAMPLES

#1	Meeting agenda	8
#2	Employee evaluation form	29
#3	New employee progress evaluation	31
#4	Time sheet	36
#5	Application form	40
#6	Education request form	62
#7	Education evaluation form	64
#8	Request for quotation	90
#9	Table of contents	94
#10	Benefits chart	96

FIGURES

#1	Hierarchical organization chart	19
#2	Non-hierarchical organization chart	19
#3	Company map	98
#4	Parking map	99

TABLES

#1	Prohibited areas of questioning in employment interviews	41

PART I
GETTING STARTED

1
WHO NEEDS A PERSONNEL MANUAL, ANYWAY?

We are glad you have decided to become a member of the (company) team. We hope your association with the company will be challenging, rewarding, and interesting.

We wish to provide opportunity and incentive for the growth and well-being of all our employees. This handbook is designed to furnish you with information about personnel administration and to answer questions that you may have concerning our everyday operations. If you have any questions that this book does not answer, don't hesitate to ask your immediate supervisor for assistance.

Our future success as a company and as individuals depends on our mutual respect and cooperation and on each of our contributions to the company's objectives. Our present position in our industry is a direct testimonial to the contributions that our employees have made in the past. Together we can make tomorrow even better. We are counting on you.

Introductory statement from a personnel manual

a. WHAT IS A PERSONNEL MANUAL?

In any society, rules develop as a natural outgrowth of a developing population. As the number of people grows, so too do the number and complexity of the interactions among the people. Rules are required to guide and govern the nature of those interactions.

Webster's Dictionary defines a society as "any organized group of people joined together because of work, interests, etc. in common." By this definition, a company is a society — whether that company is comprised of two or two thousand individuals.

Just as a society needs rules to function effectively, so does a company. Those rules frequently start out informally — we will come to work at 8:00 a.m. and leave at 5:00 p.m. — and this system works quite well for a period of time. As time elapses, however, and as the company grows or changes, the rules need to be formalized. They need to be written down.

It is that process of writing down the rules that constitutes the development of a personnel manual in its simplest form.

The role of the personnel handbook is to establish rules and guidelines by which everyone in the company can operate. The handbook provides a structure for presenting these rules as well as a source of information for employees and managers alike. It provides consistency so that employees can be assured that they will be treated fairly, and it offers an authoritative source for managers who need to know how to handle specific situations.

Within the pages of the handbook are housed not only rules, but also information on insurance benefits, vacation and holiday issues, disciplinary procedures, and any other information that is relevant to the work situations of the company personnel.

Because of the breadth of information included in the personnel manual, as well as the importance this document acquires within an organization, it also takes on certain legal connotations. For this reason, whether your handbook is a simple 2-page document or a more comprehensive 300-page tome, legal review of the completed piece — or legal involvement in its development — is advised.

b. WHY DOES MY COMPANY NEED A PERSONNEL MANUAL?

A personnel manual serves a number of purposes within an organization. It establishes the rules and guidelines by which employees will function on the job. It outlines benefits. It serves as an arbitration device in the event of disputes. It can be useful as an orientation and training tool. It can outline hiring and promotion policies as well as employee development opportunities.

By far the most important use of the manual, however, is to lay down the guidelines by which all members of the organization — your society — will operate.

By requiring the company to define and set down in concrete form its policies, the personnel handbook also helps a company work toward meeting important goals such as —

- recognizing each person as an important individual,
- establishing appropriate objectives or standards for each position within the organization,
- reviewing regularly the performance of all staff members to inform them of their status and to provide them with guidance to help them progress in their positions and in the company,
- promoting from within the company those individuals qualified to fill job vacancies or new positions,
- maintaining salary scales that compare favorably with those maintained by other companies and the local business community for similar work, and administering salaries in a manner that recognizes the relative importance of each position and rewards competent and meritorious performance,
- providing an efficient environment by maintaining good physical working conditions and by fostering harmonious relationships among employees,
- providing planned training, education, and staff development activities, and regarding them as an investment for the mutual benefit of employees and the company, and
- establishing and maintaining a truly "open-door" environment with all members of the staff to encourage open communications at all levels of employment.

For company owners, the personnel handbook should be viewed as a legal document establishing a form of contract with employees. It is your documentation that employees have, indeed, been informed of certain rules and policies, that they do know which actions are grounds for dismissal, and that they understand and agree to the terms of employment. Recognize, though, that you will want to downplay the contractual nature of the handbook for legal liability reasons. (For more on legal considerations regarding your personnel manual, see chapter 10.)

For managers as well as company owners, the personnel handbook is a repository of information — information that might otherwise be forgotten, misinterpreted, or miscommunicated. It is, for all practical purposes, the company bible.

For employees, the manual is a reference that provides information to answer their questions. Here, in one convenient, easily accessible place, employees can find answers to such questions as:

- What are the standard work hours?
- What are the paid holidays?
- What are the health benefits?
- What rules of conduct must I abide by?
- What is the dress code for my position?

In short, the personnel manual is an indispensable tool to keep your company, large or small, running smoothly. By creating and using such a reference, you ensure that everyone in the company understands the parameters of his or her job, his or her place in the overall organization, and what conduct is expected in this particular "society." With uncertainty and confusion banished, both employees and managers can do their jobs better.

2
WE'RE ALL IN THIS TOGETHER: CREATING AND WORKING WITH A TEAM

Handbook preparation should not be considered a simple matter, but neither should it be considered an insurmountable task. Depending on the size and complexity of your organization, preparation of a handbook can take anywhere from one week to several months of consideration, data gathering, group discussion, and actual preparation.

It is important to involve all associates of the company in the process by soliciting their input, sharing information, and avoiding the perception of a "secretive policy formulating society" that excludes certain members.

a. FORMING A COMMITTEE

A personnel manual should not be developed in a vacuum. By its very nature, the development of a manual suggests that you have personnel who will be affected by what goes within the pages of that book. Don't develop a handbook that is viewed as a collection of edicts coming down from above. Involve your employees in the process and you'll be able to elicit their ideas as well as their support of the final document.

The best way to do this is to create a committee or team that includes both managers or supervisors and employees. Select representatives based on their role in the organization, their understanding of corporate issues, and their ability to contribute valuable input.

Unfortunately, with a very small company, forming a committee could be difficult: one person might be all you need or can spare to work on this project. In that case, you will need to give the task to someone who is in touch with all levels in your company. If that person is a manager, make sure that he or she can elicit open, honest input from employees. If an employee, he or she should be sensitive to the requirements of management. If you use a "one-person committee," you should perhaps maintain a closer eye on the project to make sure that the "committee" doesn't go off on a personal tangent or overlook something vital.

1. Formulate the purpose of the group

You first need a statement of the purpose of the committee. The statement might be "A committee to work together toward the development of an employee handbook that will include work rules, benefit information, and conditions of employment." Be clear about what you expect from the group in terms of input and time commitment. Will the group meet once a week? Once a month? For what period of time? Will the group be advisory in nature or will they have policy formulating responsibility?

2. Announce the opportunity to serve on the committee

Next, you need to let people know that the committee is being formed and that they are welcome to submit their names. In a small company, this can be done through a regular staff meeting. Or, you might distribute a memo inviting participants or post the opportunity in the cafeteria or common room, inviting employees to sign up if they have an interest in serving. Indicate a date by which you need employees to express interest.

3. Select participants

In many cases, you may find that you can include all of those who expressed an interest in serving on the committee. Obviously this would be the optimum. If interest is too broad, however, you will need to narrow the group so the number of people working on the project is not unwieldy. Generally a group of from five to eight participants works best.

One way of broadening the number of people who can participate is to form subgroups: one group to work on benefit information, one to work on standards of conduct, etc.

Make your selection as soon as possible after the cut-off date you've established.

4. Schedule an initial meeting

Assemble the group you've selected as soon as possible to take advantage of the initial interest in the project and the momentum that has, hopefully, been established. Some of the items you might want to cover in this initial meeting include —

(a) the purpose and scope of the project (be specific about what you expect from the group — what are the deliverables?),

(b) who will be the group leader,

(c) the critical dates (deadline for submitting draft, for presenting final product, etc.),

(d) meeting times, and

(e) communication issues.

A critical task of this first meeting is selecting a group leader. Allow the group (or groups) to select its own leader. Again, that leader does not have to be (and probably shouldn't be) a representative from management.

Another critical issue is communication. How will the progress of the committee be communicated back to other members of the company? A delicate balance must be maintained. While you want to keep employees informed of what's happening, you don't want to create confusion and unnecessary concern over policies that are half-formed or simply "under consideration." Develop a communication system that will be timely and accurate and that will alleviate, as much as possible, the natural concerns that your work force will have.

Above all, don't allow the committee to operate as a "select" or "secretive" group. Committee members should be discussing what goes on at their meetings and should be soliciting additional input from employees who are not committee members. Remember, this handbook needs to be a reflection of your company and the employees who form your company. Involve, as much as possible, all members of your work force.

At the same time, be sure to communicate that decisions will be made — either by the group or by you as business owner — that some employees will not agree with. You will not be able to please everyone and that is not the goal. The goal is to gather input and make informed decisions based upon that input. Be clear about this process and you will avoid unnecessary problems later if unpopular decisions must be made.

b. WORKING TOGETHER AS A TEAM

1. What is a team?

A team is a group of people who work together with a common goal. Your handbook committee must be a team, working together with the common goal of creating a personnel manual that accurately reflects the culture, philosophies, and standards of the organization.

A good team brings more information to the group and broader perspective to the group's communications and thoughts, fosters a better understanding of what is required to achieve success, and inspires the effort required to make that success reality. Team communications and team commitment are essential to the group decision-making process.

"Too many cooks spoil the broth" often describes ineffective teams. In poorly functioning teams, conflicts can occur because of differing perceptions of what the goals of the group should be. Personalities sometimes clash or there may be a general feeling of mistrust among group members. These are some of the issues you will need to be aware of — and prepared to address — as you move forward with the development of your handbook.

Understanding how to work together effectively as a team will make the process of gathering and selecting information a less frustrating and more productive one.

2. Setting goals

Will the group you've selected be able — and willing — to work together effectively? You can make this easier by ensuring that they —

(a) clearly understand their goals and the product you are looking for,

(b) have clear direction along with well-defined leadership, and

(c) have a process in place for dealing with potential conflicts and differences in opinion.

These are critical issues that should be addressed before progress can begin. Assessing the task, determining resources, forecasting the probability of success, designing and developing a plan to achieve goals, and implementing plans at the right moment are all key elements to developing a well-functioning team.

Most important, however, is setting goals. Team members are a critical resource — each with individual skills that will be brought to bear. Before they can be effective, though, the task must be clear and reasonable. What are the expectations of the business? Of management? How do these expectations translate into goals?

In developing goals, it is important that roles and responsibilities are assigned and agreed to. The individuals on the handbook committee must share information with each other, motivate each other, and clearly know what their individual roles are within the group.

c. MEANINGFUL MEETINGS

Assuming that you have selected the right individuals to participate in the development of the personnel manual and that goals and roles have been made clear, the next step is assuring that the meetings you hold will be effective.

1. The agenda

Prepare an agenda for each meeting. It is likely that you will need to hold a series of several meetings to get the larger task of completing the handbook accomplished. But to keep the meetings focused, each individual meeting must have a purpose of its own. To define that purpose, an agenda is a critical tool.

The major cause of wasted time at meetings is poor preparation. By preparing an agenda you assure that all participants — including the group leader — know what is going to happen. You provide the meeting with a direction, a course of action.

The agenda should indicate the approximate length of the meeting, the topics to be discussed and what is expected of each of the meeting members. It should set an order for topics of discussion and establish time limits for each.

The agenda should be prepared and distributed at least one day prior to the actual meeting. Sample #1 shows a typical form of agenda.

2. Keeping minutes

Meeting minutes are another critical element in assuring that your committee will achieve its goals. Make sure that the proceedings of each meeting are recorded properly. Since this group will be dealing with issues of policy formulation, it is especially important that decisions made are accurately recorded and can be readily referred to later.

Minute taking is a task that should be shared among the committee members; each should take a turn. That way, no one person feels "saddled" with what is commonly seen as an unpleasant task. Taking minutes also sharpens your ability to listen and forces you to really understand what is being said, skills that every committee member can probably afford to improve.

For more on the art of taking minutes, see *The Minute Taker's Handbook*, another title in the Self-Counsel Series.

SAMPLE #1
MEETING AGENDA

CALL TO ORDER

ROUTINE BUSINESS

    1. Approval of the agenda

    2. Approval of the minutes of the previous meeting

    3. Communications (read by secretary)

    4. Reports

        (a) Chair

        (b) Other officers

        (c) Standing committees

        (d) Special committees

BUSINESS ARISING FROM THE PREVIOUS MEETING

or

UNFINISHED BUSINESS

    1. Item under discussion at the adjournment of the last meeting

    2. Item prompted by decision or discussion at the last meeting

NEW BUSINESS

    1. Most important or most urgent item

    2. Second most important or urgent item

    3. Third most important or urgent item

    4. Other business

ADJOURNMENT

3. Negotiating

Because the very nature of developing an employee handbook suggests that there will be issues that all members of the group — or your work force — will not agree upon, it is important that you be familiar with some sound negotiating strategies that can help you reach a consensus if possible.

Negotiation doesn't have to be a dirty word. Very often, when we think *negotiate*, we also think *winner* and *loser*. When we go into a negotiation situation, whether it be negotiating for a new piece of office equipment, the opportunity to attend a seminar, or approval for a pet project, we want to avoid "losing" — we want to "win."

The key to effective negotiation is understanding that both parties can be winners. One way to achieve this goal is to learn to listen effectively to what the other group members have to say. Listening is not a passive process. It's an active process that requires your full attention and careful consideration to the perspectives presented. Don't tune out because you don't agree with a point being made. The information provided may cause you to change or modify your initial position.

Far too many negotiators begin a negotiation by stating their case. Remember, your goal is a win-win situation. How can you assure that the other side will win if you don't know what *their* objectives are?

We often resort to compromise in a negotiation. But, without fully understanding what the goals of the other person are, no compromise can be truly effective.

Here's an example:

Two sisters are fighting over an orange. They both want the orange and neither is willing to give in. Finally, they decide on a compromise. They will cut the orange in half. This seems like a fair and equitable solution — until we discover what each sister's goal really was.

One sister wanted the pulp of the orange to eat. The other wanted the rind to use in baking a cake. Obviously, cutting the orange in half resulted in each sister getting only half of what she truly wanted. Had they explored each other's needs, they would have both received 100% of what they wanted to begin with.

As you can see, there is rarely only one alternative available in any situation. By fully exploring the goals and barriers of both sides in a negotiation, it's possible to come up with alternatives that will meet the needs of both sides.

Negotiating is an art, but one that you can practice and improve at. Among other things, you should learn to —

(a) sell the benefits,

(b) listen,

(c) ask questions,

(d) make them think it's their idea, and

(e) handle subjective objections.

(a) Sell the benefits

It's the oldest and best trick in any salesperson's arsenal. Sell to the needs of the customer. Consider how what you want will benefit the other side.

For example, if you feel strongly that a policy of two weeks' notice for vacation is important to your company, but are receiving opposition from the group, how can you convince them to see the merits of your position? By showing them how the policy benefits them.

In this case, some benefits might be that workloads can be more easily planned without undue burden placed on the workers left in the office, time-off requests are more likely to be approved with advanced notice, etc.

When presenting your positions, always formulate your presentation to focus on the benefits offered to the group.

(b) Listen

Good listening skills can't be stressed too much. Many people who are involved in negotiations fail to listen closely enough to what the other side has to say. And, in doing this, they cheat themselves out of some good information that they can put to use either in this negotiation or in future ones.

Listen for what is said as well as what is implied through body language. Listen for the objections and the basis for those objections. Try to gain some insights into what makes the other person "tick."

And, there's a benefit to listening that goes beyond the gathering of information. We all like to be listened to. You'll put yourself on solid footing with your opponent if you demonstrate a genuine interest in what he or she has to say.

(c) Ask questions

By asking questions, you not only help clarify, in your own mind, the merits of others' positions, you also help your opponents spot holes in their own arguments. In essence, you help them "talk themselves out of" their positions.

When asking questions, ask "what" as opposed to "why" questions. "What" questions are less threatening and less likely to cause defensiveness. In addition, ask open-ended questions to solicit broader responses rather than simple "yes/no" questions that really don't provide a great deal of information.

(d) Make them think it's their idea

Experienced businesspeople know that they can accomplish a great deal if they don't care who gets the credit for a good idea. One very effective way to win over people is to successfully maneuver them into thinking that it was all their idea in the first place. We're more committed to believing in and supporting ideas in which we feel ownership than we are in those that "belong" to somebody else.

(e) Handle subjective objections

You know you're going to face objections to some of the issues you will be discussing. Some objections are easy to deal with — if you have facts to back up your positions, simply present them. Other objections will be more subjective: "I don't think that's a good policy idea."

One of the best ways to deal with this kind of subjective objection is simply to acknowledge the validity of your opponent's point and move on to another issue. For example: "I can understand why you say the two-week vacation notice might be a negative for some employees. Now let me tell you why I think this policy will actually benefit the work force."

4. Dealing with defensiveness

Meetings, with their rapid and complex interplay of personalities and personal strategies, can bring out characteristics in people that remain hidden under less stressful circumstances. Some people may become overly aggressive, shouting down others' comments. On the other hand, many people feel threatened by this kind of group situation or by having their opinions questioned by other committee members.

People who feel threatened often react with defensiveness. Unfortunately, two people engaged in a discussion or argument may each feel threatened by the other and begin to act defensively, and two defensive people will not be able to communicate effectively. One of these people must be able to recognize what is happening, take charge of the situation, and accept responsibility for defusing the defensiveness.

Defensiveness is most often demonstrated by observable behaviors — behaviors that we all find familiar. Some of the most common signs are —

(a) lack of eye contact,

(b) glaring,

(c) raised voice,

(d) flared nostrils,

(e) flushed face,

(f) withdrawal,

(g) finger-pointing (literally),

(h) quick disagreement,

(i) sarcasm, and

(j) slamming objects or throwing things.

Certain statements or actions are bound to provoke defensiveness in others. Some examples:

- "You're wrong."
- "That's not true."
- "Why are you so (insert appropriate word)."
- "Why are you being so defensive?"
- "That's stupid!"
- "You're crazy."
- "You misunderstand me."
- "What's the matter with you?"

No doubt you could add to the list. There are other non-verbal "people arousers" that have the same effect. Some of these include walking away, rolling the eyes, smiling with a sneer, or shaking one's head. The message regarding these kind of "hackle-raising" comments or actions is simple: don't.

Whether you hear yourself or someone else using provoking words, or notice yourself or a colleague showing physical signs of a defensive attitude, it is up to you to take action. Good communication is a key to completing your task of developing the personnel handbook, as well as in distributing and supporting the material contained within the handbook, and defensiveness blocks communication.

Following are some tips that can help you avoid or deal with defensiveness:

(a) Be aware of your personal "hot spots." What are your personal ego-deflaters? What kinds of things can people say to you that immediately make you see red? Once you've identified your personal "hot spots," decide how you'll react productively rather than defensively to these in the future.

(b) Be aware of your defensive signals. What are some of the things you do when you start to become defensive? In most cases you won't be personally aware of your defensive reactions. The best way to find out is to ask those you deal with often.

Only by becoming aware of your own defensive signals can you work at overcoming them. Defensiveness is a reciprocal problem. If you appear defensive, you'll provoke a defensive reaction. When you receive a defensive reaction, your first impulse is to respond defensively... and on it goes.

(c) Avoid "you" statements. Take responsibility for the conversation. Instead of saying, "You don't understand me," you might say, "I must not be making myself clear," or "I'm not explaining this very well; let me try again." By taking responsibility, in essence taking "the blame," you can avoid damaging the ego or self-worth of the person you're communicating with and, hopefully, avoid a defensive response.

(d) Keep an open mind. Communicating effectively means keeping an open mind when hearing things you may not like. It means not rejecting someone's ideas simply because you disagree with them. Along with this goes a certain measure of self-control. Even if you control the impulse to disagree verbally, you may still be arguing silently. You need to try to keep an open mind — verbally and non-verbally.

(e) Understand that rational minds can differ. Other people's ideas make sense to them even if they don't to you. Remind yourself of this when you're involved in a confrontation with someone. You can always "agree to disagree." There's rarely, if ever, any point in trying to force someone to agree with your point of view.

(f) Don't interrupt. When you're in the middle of a confrontation with someone who is responding defensively, it's important to resist the impulse to interrupt and interject your own perceptions. If you don't take time to listen, further communication will be hopeless.

PART II
CONSIDERING YOUR CONTENT

3
CREATING AN OUTLINE

Once a committee has been established and an initial meeting has been held for organizational purposes, the next step is to decide exactly what will be included in the handbook.

There is no magical list of what should or should not be included. The items outlined in this book are designed to be a guide that can help you identify items you want to include, exclude, or consider for possible inclusion in the future. Your handbook is a reflection of your corporate culture. It's contents will depend on the size, nature, and background of your company and your employees.

Creating an outline for your personnel manual will be an ongoing process. You will need a general outline before gathering any information, to provide a roadmap for the group of where you are going and to help direct your efforts in terms of what information you will ultimately need.

Your outline should develop as you proceed, as you fill in "holes" and a more complete outline suggests itself.

After all information has been gathered, finalizing the outline should be a simple process of organizing the information in a logical manner and noting major sections with specific items that are contained in each.

a. WHAT DO I NEED TO INCLUDE?

For your initial information-gathering process, you will need some idea of what kinds of topics are appropriate for a personnel manual. The following general outline of topics will help you get started. Of course, you may not want to include all of these areas in your company's manual. On the other hand, your discussions and research may point out topics not listed here that are of great importance to your particular situation. Use this list as a guide while seeking information and gathering input, then develop your own customized outline as you proceed.

The company
- Mission statement
- Corporate philosophy
- Organizational chart
- Job descriptions

Issues of pay and performance
- Performance reviews
- Salary reviews
- Employee classifications
- Changes in employee status
- Issues of pay
- Outside employment (moonlighting)
- Reimbursement for expenses
- Use of personal automobiles (mileage per diem)
- Work hours
- Hours of operation
- Attendance policies
- Hiring policies
- Hiring relatives

- Reduction in staff
- Exit interviews
- References
- Termination

Benefits
- Vacation
- Jury duty
- Military leave
- Funeral leave
- Doctor and dental appointments
- Holidays
- Sick leave
- Personal leave
- Family and medical leave
- General leaves of absence
- Health insurance
- Life insurance
- Disability income
- Dental insurance
- Extended benefits after leaving the company (e.g., pensions)
- Sharing of company profits
- Worker's compensation
- Unemployment compensation
- Employee education
- Employee-assistance program

Standards of conduct
- Problem resolution
- Disciplinary procedures
- Disciplinary appeals process
- Voluntary termination
- Involuntary termination

General information
- Telephone procedures
- Business gifts
- Personal property
- Company property
- Contributions for gifts
- Other contributions
- Personal mail
- Smoking/chewing tobacco
- Company vehicles
- Automobile liability coverage
- Seat belts
- Traffic tickets and parking violations
- Alcohol on company premises or on business travel
- Confidential nature of business
- Personnel records
- Sexual harassment

b. GATHERING INFORMATION

One of the earliest steps in deciding what will go into your manual is gathering information from a number of sources. The information gathered will determine the outline and organization of the handbook.

Much of the information you will include already exists in the form of memos, procedures, benefit information, and miscellaneous information that is "understood." For instance, it may be an "unwritten policy" that employees are expected to report to work at a certain time. Another unwritten policy may be that the office shuts down on Good Friday and Easter Monday.

The first step in data gathering is to collect all the written materials that currently exist. Poke around and ask questions. Have there been any earlier abortive attempts to write a personnel manual? Who has copies of policy-setting memos? Are company benefit policies set out in any literature provided by the insurer? Does the office manager approve vacation schedules according to a clever formula she scribbled down at a management seminar? All this information will prove useful in your project.

The next step, and one that may take longer, is to spend some time discussing what your company's "unwritten policies" are. Select a record keeper to record these items. Remember to talk to all levels of company associates, not just to managers.

Preparing a list of questions to guide your discussions is a good idea. After all, you have a number of different topics to raise with each person. Just walking up to someone and saying, "So, what do you think the unwritten policies of the company are?" would likely elicit a blank stare. Most people will require some prompting. For example, to introduce the topic of dress codes, you might say, "What kinds of clothes would you consider inappropriate for someone in your position?"

Your data-gathering activities may very well extend beyond the boundaries of your own organization. It can be very helpful to review the handbooks of other organizations for ideas on the types of information to include as well as on how to organize and lay out the handbook. While each company is unique, there are certain standards that are common to many companies and your efforts can be speeded along substantially by borrowing information and ideas from handbooks that are already in existence.

To obtain access to others' personnel handbooks, you can —

- speak to your colleagues or networking contacts who work at other companies. They will be glad to share information with you.

- contact personnel or human resource associations. You may already be a member of appropriate groups. If not, you can obtain leads through directories such the *Encyclopedia of Associations* published by Gale Research Company, Book Tower, Detroit, Michigan, 48226, 1-800-223-GALE.

- call companies directly and ask to speak to the human resources/personnel manager. Explain that you're in the process of developing a personnel manual and would be interested in reviewing their materials for ideas and direction. You'll find that many companies will be very willing to help you out, not only with copies of their materials, but with helpful tips from their own experience that can help you as you proceed with your task.

When you feel that your information gathering is complete, review all of the material to determine —

(a) whether it is still valid,

(b) whether it should be included in the handbook, and

(c) whether additional data gathering will need to be done.

Creating an outline can be time-consuming since this process will engender a great deal of discussion among the committee members. For example: "Do we want to outline a disciplinary process?" "What should that process be?" Certain issues will be more controversial than others and the group may need to spend some time coming to a consensus.

While company owners and top management will probably have the final say on what to include in the handbook, it is important to allow the committee the flexibility to make the initial recommendations. This input will be valuable to you in determining what you will ultimately include and how you will formulate and document certain policies and procedures.

4
THE COMPANY

The personnel manual is a great place to introduce employees to your company, both in terms of your company background and in terms of your company's philosophies or "culture."

Culture is a critical part of any organization. Every company has a distinctive "corporate culture" whether the company leaders realize it or not. Corporate culture can be defined as "those values peculiar to an organization that direct and control the decisions and flow of work through it."

Culture evolves as a company grows. It evolves to combat the kinds of inconsistencies that can be threatening to employees. A good corporate culture contributes to stability and consistency, which, in turn, make employees feel secure.

Fostering a corporate culture is not a simple process. In fact, the shaping of culture does not remain totally within the control of the company. Corporate culture is going to happen. It's built by small decision after small decision, year after year.

However, your personnel handbook can play a vital role in establishing corporate culture.

a. THE MISSION STATEMENT

Many companies include in their handbooks a formal statement of corporate culture. This statement is often referred to as a "mission" or "vision" statement. Here are some examples:

> NSP will be the quality provider of electric, gas, and energy-related services in the region. We will continually improve the value of our products and services for our customers. We will enhance our opportunities for success and growth by balancing the needs of customers and shareholders, valuing our employees, supporting our communities, and protecting the environment.

* * *

> XYZ Clothing will provide quality, reasonably priced clothing for professional women, with an emphasis on service that is beyond reproach.

* * *

> Our mission is to be an innovative and customer-responsive provider of law-related information using multiple formats.

A mission statement provides employees with a framework within which to apply all of the subsequent rules and procedures contained in the manual. This framework also extends beyond the written page to encompass day-to-day activities and relationships with peers, managers, subordinates, customers, and vendors.

Your corporate mission statement should not be developed without careful consideration to the message you wish to convey. At the same time, it should be a reflection of reality and not an ivory-tower statement that has no basis in fact. Employees will quickly see through a flowery mission statement that says: "this is how we'd like to be" or "this is how we should be," instead of "this is how we are."

b. CORPORATE PHILOSOPHY

Each company has certain corporate objectives related to how it will interact with employees, customers, and the community in which it resides. These corporate objectives need to be communicated to the employees of the organization and, of course, the handbook is a key place to do just that.

Corporate objectives can be summarized in the handbook in the form of a "corporate philosophy":

> The primary objectives of the company are to —
>
> (a) have a well-organized, well-managed, productive company that can make a profitable contribution to our customers and to society;
>
> (b) produce and market products that are timely, accurate, and of value to our customers;
>
> (c) be fair, honest, and ethical in dealing with our suppliers, customers, and employees;
>
> (d) be always in pursuit of innovation — new products, new ideas, and new processes that will benefit the company, our employees, and our customers; and
>
> (e) do everything in our power to make the company a good place to work and an asset to our home community.
>
> This philosophy is a guide to thinking, and not necessarily a guide to specific action. While rules and procedures tell you what is to be done, these policies will guide you in making a decision but will leave the actual decision up to you. In other words, they leave some room for individual discretion rather than spelling out the specific actions that characterize rules and procedures.
>
> In analyzing the focus and quality of your actions, ask: Is this the way I would like to be treated? Am I doing what seems fair if I were the customer? Is this in the best interests of the company? The only thing that stands in the way of success is the ability each of us has to apply these guiding policies as we make our decisions as part of the company team. We will all be judged by the quality of our decisions.

c. THE ORGANIZATIONAL CHART

Another critical clue to the operation of any company is the organizational chart. This diagram provides employees — old and new — with an idea of where they fit in. Who has authority over them? Who do they have authority over? Who are their peers? What are the reporting lines? Where can they move within the organization — what are the lines of advancement? These are just a few of the critical questions that can be answered through your organizational chart.

An organizational chart is nothing more than a graphic depiction of reporting lines (see Figure #1). The typical organizational chart shows a top-down progression from the president or CEO to the "people on the front lines."

Today, many companies are moving away from this hierarchical depiction and are designing organizational charts that have a more circular structure which, they feel, connotes teamwork and takes the emphasis off hierarchy (see Figure #2). Whichever format you choose, the elements will be the same.

FIGURE #1
HIERARCHICAL ORGANIZATION CHART

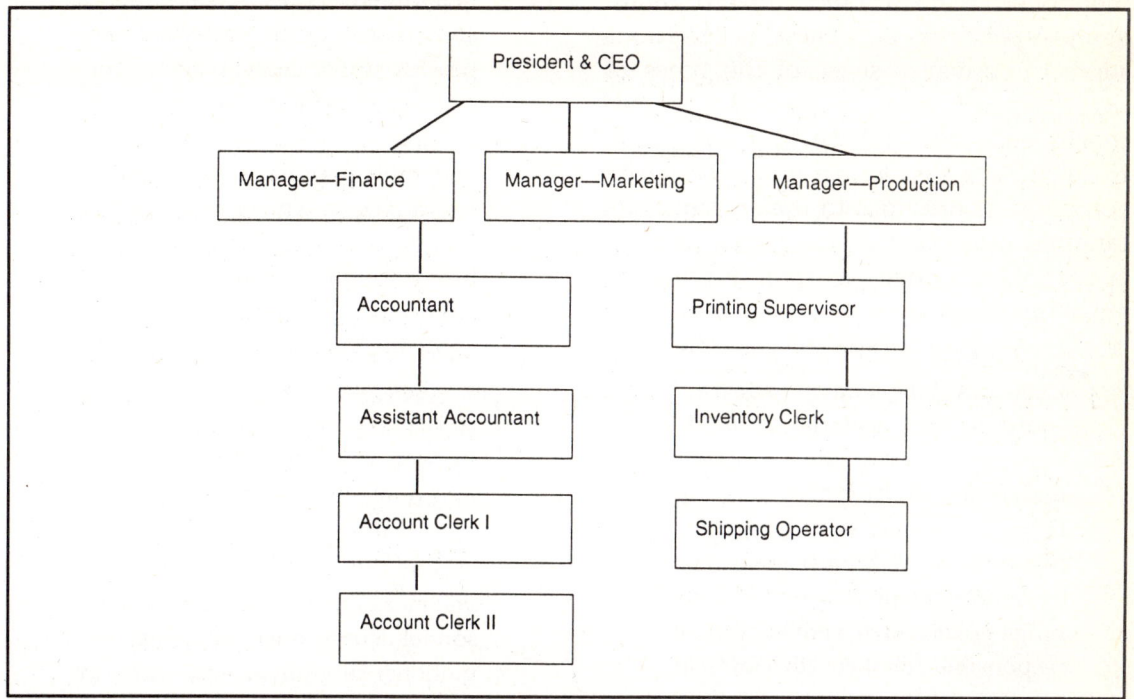

FIGURE #2
NON-HIERARCHICAL ORGANIZATION CHART

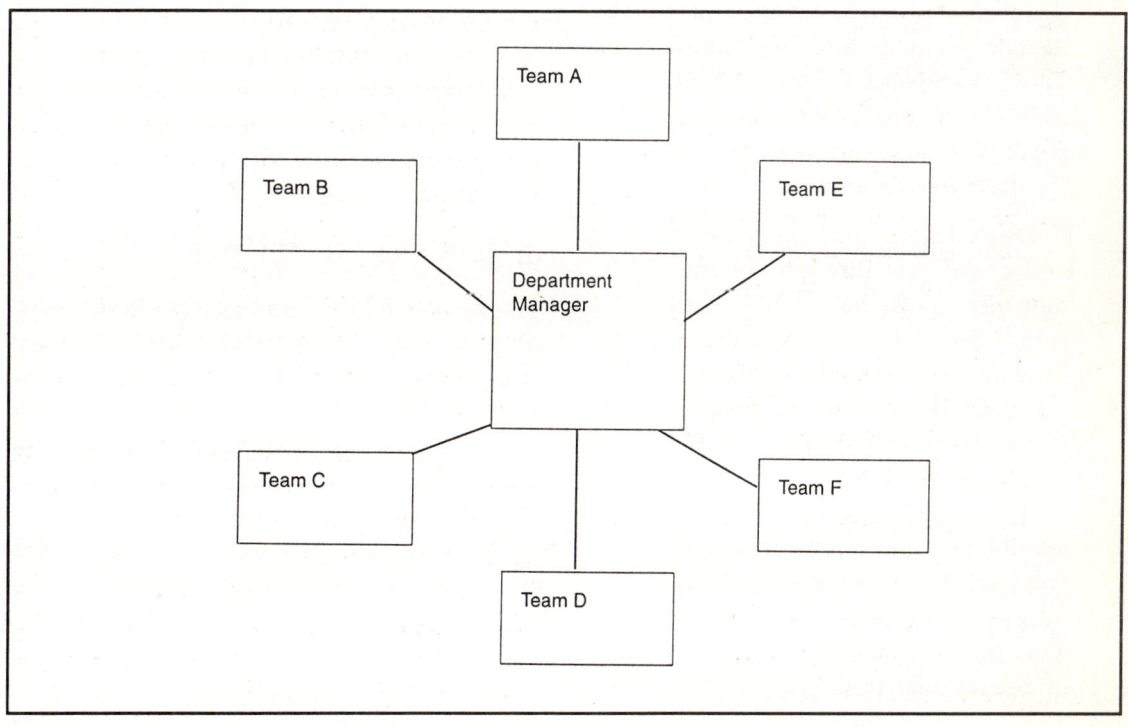

You may also want to include in your handbook written descriptions that outline the responsibilities of each type of position mentioned — for instance, director, manager, supervisor, etc. These descriptions serve to convey a sense of the types of decisions each position can make, the authority each has, and the way these positions interact with others within the company. It provides to the employees a tangible indication of the rights and responsibilities conveyed upon the managers of the company as well as an indication of where to go with specific concerns.

Directors of the company direct and coordinate the activities of the departments within their divisions and/or aid the president in formulating and administering organization policies. They participate in the development of long- and short-range goals and objectives, and are responsible for their division's attainment of those goals and objectives. Directors review analyses of departmental activities, costs, operations, and forecast information to determine progress toward their divisions' goals and objectives. They are responsible for the hiring, training, and review of positions reporting to them, and they serve on the Executive Committee.

Department managers direct and coordinate through subordinate personnel the activities and functions of their departments. They utilize knowledge of department functions, company policies, and standards and practices in the performance of their duties. They assign or delegate responsibility for specific work tasks. They also give work directions, resolve problems, prepare work schedules, and set deadlines to ensure the completion of operational functions in their departments. Managers coordinate the activities of their departments with interrelated activities of other departments. They prepare reports and records on department activities for upper management. They evaluate current departmental procedures and practices and develop and implement alternative methods for the improvement of work flow and productivity. Managers do all hiring, training, performance evaluation, and discipline for positions reporting to them.

Assistant managers are responsible for the effective and efficient operation of a distinct functional unit within a department. They supervise the daily activities of associates involved in the same function and make recommendations on personnel actions such as hiring, promotions, discipline, and wage increases. They are also responsible for the training and performance evaluation of associates reporting to them. Assistant managers analyze and resolve work problems in their functional area, evaluate procedures and recommend improvements, and keep records and prepare reports on their activities for upper management.

d. JOB DESCRIPTIONS

The next level of detail is the job description. The job description is an objective way of defining the tasks performed on a job as well as the skills necessary to perform those tasks. It is a written record of the job that outlines the tasks and responsibilities involved and indicates how the particular job ties in with others in the company. The job description typically consists of —

(a) job identification,

(b) job summary, and

(c) job duties.

The job identification includes the title of the position, the date the job description was prepared, the title of the position's immediate supervisor, and, if relevant, whether the position is exempt (i.e., management) or non-exempt (i.e., nonmanagement).

The job summary is a brief description of the job highlighting the general responsibilities and characteristics of the work performed.

The most important section, job duties, describes the specific tasks of the position, including information on what each duty is, how it should be performed, and why.

As you write the job descriptions, be sure to —

(a) indicate the frequency or degree of duties performed (e.g., daily, weekly, monthly, etc.);

(b) be specific, avoid generalities;

(c) start each statement with an action verb (e.g., *operate, report, direct*),

(d) use short phrases — don't worry about using complete sentences;

(e) list major responsibilities first and other responsibilities in descending order of importance;

(f) enlist the help of the employee in developing the job description or job standards; and

(g) include that all-important catch phrase: "any other duties as required."

If you have a small organization, you may decide to include all job descriptions in your employee handbook. In a larger company, this may not be practical; however, you can still include a section on how job descriptions are developed and modified as well as information on where employees might obtain copies of their job description.

Job descriptions are the basis for our evaluation and salary systems. Therefore, it is very important to keep them current. In order to do this, these documents are to be reviewed at each of your performance appraisals. This is your opportunity to make sure your job description is accurate. Changes are to be indicated on your current job description. If you do not have a copy of your current job description, you may obtain one from your manager or from the Human Resources Manager.

Once completed, the job description offers an objective indication of the responsibilities and requirements of a particular position. It is the final step in providing a clear indication to employees of where and how they fit into the organization.

**Job Description —
Manager, Customer Accounting**

Position summary

Managerial and administrative responsibility associated with the customer business office operations of the company. Functional areas of responsibility include customer accounting and billing, credit and collections, and response to customer inquiries.

Requirements

Accounting/business degree with a minimum of five years' experience in the customer service and general accounting areas of the company. A thorough knowledge and understanding of the business and customer services operations of the company is required.

Essential functions

(1) Provide direction and support to the outlying customer offices in the areas of customer accounting and

billing, credit and collections, and customer inquiries.

(2) Manage the development and implementation of the policies and procedures pertaining to customer accounting and billing, credit and collections, and customer inquiries.

(3) Manage, develop, and conduct evaluation processes.

(4) Manage the development and coordination of enhancements associated with the Customer Information System (CIS) and the Credit Management System (CMS).

(5) Responsible for hiring, training, evaluation, and discipline of employees that report to this position.

Job description —
Advertising Assistant

Job summary

Assist in the development, creation, and production of advertising materials.

Job duties and responsibilities

Major duties:

- Proofread and edit all promotional materials
- Compose space advertisements
- Maintain and update media information files
- Monitor effectiveness of promotional activities

Minor duties:

- Input in-house memos, reports, and other materials as needed
- Compile information and prepare reports as requested
- Other job-related duties as assigned by supervisor

Organizational relationships

Directly accountable to advertising manager. Works closely with the graphic design department in the preparation of ads and other promotional materials.

e. WHO IS NOT COVERED BY LABOR STANDARDS LAW?

In both the United States and Canada, certain workers are not covered by some employment standards legislation. Whether a particular position in your company is exempted is important to the employees, so the fact should be mentioned in your handbook either in the specific job descriptions or in a general discussion at some point.

1. Exempt vs. nonexempt employees — U.S. law

In the United States, one of the areas where companies typically run into trouble is determining the distinction between exempt and nonexempt workers. This distinction is important because exempt employees are excluded from minimum-wage and overtime rules due to the nature of their job responsibilities. Nonexempt employees are covered by all provisions of the act.

Don't fall prey to the common misconception that hourly employees are automatically nonexempt and salaried employees are exempt. This is not the case. An employee's status depends on job duties — not titles or pay classifications.

There are four categories of jobs that are exempt:

(a) Executive

(b) Administrative

(c) Professional

(d) Outside sales

For an executive exemption, the employee must —

(a) manage an enterprise, department, or subdivision as a primary duty,

(b) direct the work of at least two full-time employees,

(c) have authority to hire and fire or make recommendations on the same, and

(d) spend no more than 20% of work time on non-managerial duties.

For an administrative exemption, the employee must —

(a) either be responsible for office work directly related to management or general operations or be responsible for work directly related to academic instruction or training at a school;

(b) regularly exercise discretion and individual judgment, as opposed to merely following procedures, and have authority to make important decisions;

(c) regularly assist an owner or executive, or perform work that requires special training or experience under only general supervision, or work on special assignment under general supervision;

(d) spend at least 80% of work time on administrative duties; and

(e) make at least $155 a week exclusive of room and board.

For a professional exemption, the employee must perform work that —

(a) requires knowledge of advanced type in field of science or learning;

(b) is original and creative in a recognized field of artistic endeavor; or

(c) involves imparting knowledge as a certified or recognized teacher.

For an outside sales exemption, the employee must customarily and regularly work away from the employer's premises in making sales or obtaining orders or contracts. This exempt work includes work incidental to and in conjunction with outside sales, such as incidental deliveries and collections.

It is probably better if you do not include these definitions of the classifications in your personnel handbook since they are somewhat ambiguous and open to interpretation. The exempt/non-exempt distinction is a gray one and prone to controversy. Simply include wording similar to the following paragraphs to distinguish between exempt and nonexempt employees in your personnel manual:

> **Exempt employees** do not receive overtime pay for working over 40 hours in a week (they are exempt from overtime). Exempt status is determined by job responsibilities and the provisions of the Fair Labor Standards Act.
>
> **Nonexempt employees** receive overtime pay for hours compensated over 40 in a 1-week period (Sunday through Saturday). This status is also determined by job responsibilities and the Fair Labor Standards Act.

The guidelines that help you determine an employee's exempt or nonexempt status are general, to say the least, and obviously open to interpretation. The safe route is to err on the side of classifying an employee as nonexempt. When in doubt, go that route. Otherwise, consult with your lawyer or legal adviser.

2. Labor standards legislation — Canadian law

In Canada, the law also commonly distinguishes between certain workers who are covered by the labor standards legislation and those who are not. However, the exact categories of exempted workers vary from province to province. In British Columbia and Ontario, for example, most professionals such as foresters, doctors, dentists, and veterinarians are among those exempted. People employed on fishing boats or as police officers or farm workers may not receive the same protections as other employees under provincial legislation.

Because of the different standards among the provinces, you should obtain current and accurate information on the labor standards law in your province. Self-Counsel Press publishes *Employee/Employer Rights* guides for British Columbia and Ontario; if you live in those provinces, you may wish to consult one of those books for more information. Information on labor law should also be available from the ministry responsible for labor in your province.

If you employ any workers who are exempt from general labor standards, you should make their status clear in your personnel handbook and explain exactly what their duties and rights are.

f. EMPLOYMENT STATUS

1. Defining employment status

When you are discussing the rights and duties of employees, you need to distinguish between full-time, part-time, and temporary employment status. For example, an employee hired temporarily to do a job may not be entitled to the same benefits as someone hired full time on an ongoing basis to do the same job.

Full-time associates — (nonexempt, hourly or salaried) An associate who is regularly scheduled to work at least 30 hours a week is considered to be full time and is eligible for all company-sponsored benefits including insurance coverage and holiday, vacation, sick, and personal time off with pay. Time-off benefits will be prorated to the actual hours regularly scheduled per week for those working less than 40 hours but more than 30 hours in a week (75% or 80% time).

Full-time associates — (exempt, salaried) All full-time exempt associates (in most cases, salaried) are expected to work as scheduled. There is some flexibility in this method of compensation since exempt associates are expected to get their jobs done with a minimum amount of supervision.

It is understood that full-time exempt associates will put in whatever amount of time is necessary to accomplish their job duties. Time at work should average at least 40 hours per week. It is expected that full-time exempt associates will not abuse the inherent flexibility of their positions. Full-time exempt associates are eligible for all company-sponsored benefits.

Part-time associates — (nonexempt, hourly) An associate who works an average of less than 30 hours a week is considered part time. Part-time associates should be flexible in the hours they can work to accommodate slow and busy periods. The number of hours to be worked on a weekly basis cannot be guaranteed unless specifically arranged with your manager. If you work a variable schedule, it is your responsibility to check with your manager in advance and to know when you are to report to work. There are no company-sponsored benefits for part-time associates except vacation pay.

Temporary associates — An employee who is hired with the understanding that his or her employment will be terminated on a specific date or upon completion of a specific assignment is a temporary associate. Temporary associates are not eligible for any company-sponsored benefits. Temporary associates are to use company time sheets or time cards to record hours worked.

2. Changes in employment status

Employees may change status in your company through a number of means: going from part time to full time, going from full time to part time, going from temporary employment to continuing employment, etc. Each of these changes affect the level of benefits received and you will want to indicate in your handbook exactly how these changes affect benefits. The following examples indicate the type of wording you might want to use.

Going from temporary to continuing: Health, life, short- and long-term disability, and dental insurance benefits will be effective the first of the month following your continuing employment effective date. Vacation, sick, and personal time will begin accruing on your new anniversary date as if you were a new full-time associate.

Going from part time to full time: Health, life, short- and long-term disability, and dental insurance benefits will be effective the first of the month following your full-time effective date. If you were employed for less than six months before going full time, you will not receive vacation pay. If you have worked part time for more than six months and then go to full time, part-time vacation pay up to your new anniversary date will be determined by the formula described in the vacation pay for part-time associates. This will be paid on your next payroll check. Vacation, sick, and personal time will begin accruing on your new anniversary date as if you were a new full-time associate. See your manager regarding accelerated vacation accruals available to long-term part-time associates who have gone to full-time status.

Length of service will determine this.

Going from full time to part time: Changes to your full-time status have an effect on the benefits available to you in terms of time off and insurances. A change in your status from full time to part time will affect your insurance benefits the most. Our insurance carriers require that you work at least an average of 30 hours a week to be eligible. If you go to part time, your eligibility ends the day your status changes. You are able to continue your health and/or dental insurance, but at your complete cost. Time off and paid holiday benefits would also end at this time. You will be paid for any earned but unused vacation and personal time available to you.

Going from full time to 75% or 80% time: A change from full time to 75% or 80% time will not affect your insurance benefits, as you would still be working an average of at least 30 hours a week. Time-off benefits earned but not used will still be available to you, but your future accrual rate will be reduced to 75% or 80% of the regular rate. Holidays would be paid at 6 or 6.4 hours respectively instead of 8 hours.

Temporary reduction of hours: A temporary reduction of your hours from full time to part time or 75% or 80% time is permissible only with your Director's and the Human Resources Manager's approval. As long as you will work an average of 30 hours a week during the course of the calendar year in which your temporary reduction occurs, it will not affect your insurance eligibility. Paid time-off benefits may be reduced during the period of reduction, depending on the length of time involved and the average number of hours worked. If you anticipate the need to reduce your hours temporarily, it is important that you discuss the situation fully with your manager and the Human Resources Manager as far in advance of the occurrence as possible.

5
EMPLOYEE EVALUATIONS

Employees expect and deserve fair, comprehensive, and regular reviews of their job performance. Employee evaluation offers an opportunity for both employee and manager to discuss performance issues and to establish goals for the next review period. Evaluation is used to —

- translate corporate goals into individual objectives,
- determine salary increases and promotions,
- provide documentation for termination decisions,
- identify training needs, and
- assess employee potential.

Appraisals benefit the employer by providing control of the work, allowing for greater confidence in employees and offering the opportunity for better relationships with employees.

Employees benefit from a clear understanding of what is expected of them, recognition for their efforts, a feeling of participation in decisions that affect them, specific information on how they should improve, and a realistic idea of their own strengths and weaknesses.

Obviously, the issue of how they will be evaluated and how often is important to employees, so a discussion of exactly how your company will conduct evaluations is an important part of the personnel manual. Employees will want to know the details of when and how they will be reviewed, what standards their reviews will be based on, and how their reviews will affect their salaries. In your handbook, include copies of any forms that are used in the evaluation process, such as the evaluation form shown in Sample #2. These could form an appendix to the manual.

Performance reviews are handled differently at different companies. How you conduct reviews will depend on the type of business you operate, the number of employees you have, and your own personal preferences. In general, though, it is a good idea to have reviews on a regularly scheduled basis. Many companies choose an annual review schedule, while some opt for twice-a-year reviews. Some companies have even found quarterly reviews to be beneficial. Shorter term periods are always preferable, but given time constraints at most companies, not usually used. Often, new employees are evaluated after their probationary period (see Sample #3).

The employee evaluation is an opportunity for manager and employee to compare notes on progress during a given period of time. For a review to be effective, it is critical that employees are aware, up front, of the criteria they will be judged upon. This includes not only intangibles such as quality of work, but also specific goals that have been established cooperatively between you and your employees.

Reviews should cover objective behaviors. Rating employees on subjective standards such as "attitude" only creates problems. What is a bad attitude? To avoid no-win battles with employees over the use of such judgmental statements, focus your reviews on objective behaviors. For instance, a bad attitude might be exhibited by tardiness, inappropriate displays of anger, etc. These are the issues that should be addressed, not "attitude."

Similarly, be careful about discussing poor performance unless you can provide specific examples of what you mean. And, unless you have indicated previously to the employee the level of performance you expect and how it will be exhibited, you may find yourself responding to such objections as: "You didn't tell me I had to do that!" or "I had no idea that was part of my job!"

The key is communication. Be clear with employees in terms of what you expect from them. Be specific. If you're dealing with a production function, your job may be simplified. "We expect you to produce XXX widgets per hour at a reject rate of .001." When dealing with "knowledge workers," your task will be more difficult.

Work together with your employees to establish measurable goals that are challenging yet attainable. Then when review time come, you'll find that your job is much easier and you'll avoid unnecessary conflict and potential liability.

The review also serves as an opportunity to address employee development issues. What additional training does the employee feel he or she needs to perform better in the job? Is the employee interested in advancement? Into what areas? What additional training or skills will be required to make this advancement possible?

And, of course, you'll want to solicit feedback from the employee on how *you're* doing. Are you providing enough information? Are you available enough? Do you give clear direction? Do you hinder their output in any way?

While many managers dread reviews, if handled effectively through involvement of the employee in the establishment of clear, quantifiable goals; ongoing communication; and an honest desire to help the employee succeed on the job, you'll find that reviews can be a very rewarding part of your job.

Following is one example of a general discussion on employee evaluation that is appropriate to a personnel manual:

> The purpose of the performance appraisal process is to provide you with the opportunity to openly discuss with your manager how you can utilize your talents and abilities to their fullest and help the company reach its goals. Performance appraisal is intended to be a positive experience for you and should be approached with that attitude. You will review your past accomplishments, analyze your current performance, and plan for future activities and improvements in how you do your job.
>
> Performance appraisal is a continual process and is conducted informally by your manager on a regular basis. Formal reviews are conducted annually with six-month "check-ups." You are entitled to a copy of your review forms after they have been approved. The originals are kept in the central personnel files in Human Resources. Blank copies of all forms appear in Appendix A.

SAMPLE #2
EMPLOYEE EVALUATION FORM

EMPLOYEE EVALUATION FORM

Associate name _____

Department _____

Position _____

Date of hire _____

Date of transfer _____

Review period _____

Reviewed by _____

Date _____

| **Performance factors** | **Comments** | **Rate 1-5** |

Quantity of work _____
_____
_____
_____   _____

Quality of work _____
_____
_____
_____   _____

Internal relationships _____
_____
_____
_____   _____

External relationships (where applicable) _____
_____
_____
_____   _____

Problem-solving/decision-making ability _____
_____
_____
_____   _____

SAMPLE #2 — Continued

Other factors that may affect performance: versatility; job knowledge; communication skills; interest in job; reliability and punctuality; cost consciousness; business ethics; initiative; creativity/innovation; safety

_____
_____
_____ _____

                                                         OVERALL RATING: _____

Performance rating definitions:

Superior (25-30): Associate excels in practically all aspects of the job, having reached the highest level of job performance on a consistent basis.

Commendable (19-24): Performance exceeds criteria or standards of performance for practically all aspects of the work.

Full (13-18): Performance fully meets criteria or standards of performance for some aspects of the work, but there is a need to make a concentrated effort to improve performance in other aspects of the work.

Needs improvement (7-12): Performance meets the criteria or standards of performance for some aspects of the work but there is a need to make a concentrated effort to improve performance in other aspects of the work.

Unacceptable (1-6): Performance is well below criteria or standards of performance for almost all aspects of the work. Drastic improvements must be made immediately or retention of the associate in this job is not warranted.

Comments (general comments; performance-related areas not enumerated; performance improvement plans; etc.): _____
_____

Associate's signature* _____ Date _____

Appraiser's signature _____ Date _____

Associate's response to appraisal _____
_____
_____

*Signature does not indicate agreement by associate. It only acknowledges that the appraisal has been discussed.

SAMPLE #3
NEW EMPLOYEE PROGRESS EVALUATION

NEW EMPLOYEE PROGRESS EVALUATION

Associate name _____

Department _____

Position _____

Date of hire _____

Review period to _____

To the appraiser:

This report is to be completed after a new associate's first three months on the job. Review the completed report with your supervisor before you present it to the associate. Discuss your ratings with the associate and make any specific comments on the back of this form. At this point, you should begin the process of setting and monitoring goals and objectives for the associate.

Use the following ratings for each item:

E = Exceeds expectations

M = Meets expectations

D = Does not meet expectations

	Rating
JOB KNOWLEDGE — Understanding of skills and/or knowledge need to do the job	_____
QUALITY OF WORK — Accuracy, thoroughness, completeness of work assigned/performed	_____
QUANTITY — Output of work considering newness in position	_____
UNDERSTANDING — Ability to learn, grasp concepts essential to the work, and follow instructions/procedures	_____
COOPERATION — Ability to work well with coworkers, management, and subordinates	_____
CUSTOMERS — Understanding of their importance to us, demonstration of concern for them	_____
SUITABILITY — The person matches the job as demonstrated by attitude, personality, and temperament	_____

SAMPLE #3 — Continued

Rating

STANDARDS — Ethics, honesty, acceptance of doing business the company way _____

ATTENDANCE — (M or D only) _____

PUNCTUALITY — (M or D only) _____

Associate signature _____ Date _____

Appraiser signature _____ Date _____

Supervisor of appraiser _____ Date _____

6
ISSUES OF MONEY AND HOURS OF WORK

State, provincial, and federal regulations exist that govern the issues of salary and hours. Being familiar with the regulations that affect your business can save you a lot of trouble — and money. Small businesses have just as much accountability for abiding by the requirements of fair labor and pay laws as do large corporations. No matter what the size of your business, you don't need a lawsuit from an employee who feels he or she was badly treated.

To avoid this, make clear, legal, fair policies and put them in your personnel manual so all employees understand them.

a. THE NITTY-GRITTY PAY ISSUES

There are a number of basic issues regarding pay that your employees will want to know about. Following are some examples of these and how you might cover them in your handbook.

1. How often am I paid?

Pay periods run for two weeks beginning on a Sunday and ending on a Saturday. Paychecks for that period are distributed the following Friday (usually by noon). If a payday is a national holiday, checks will be distributed on the Thursday of that week. Paychecks are distributed by your manager.

2. What about overtime?

Overtime will be paid to all nonexempt employees (part-time and full-time) at the rate of 1½ times your regular pay rate for all hours compensated over 40 in a 1-week period (Sunday through Saturday). Any paid hours in a week taken off due to illness, vacation, or personal time will be used in computing hours for that week.

3. Do I get paid more for working on holidays?

Working on regular paid holidays is strongly discouraged. If, however, it is absolutely necessary, overtime will be paid at 1½ times your regular rate of pay. This is in addition to your regular holiday pay if you are full time.

4. Do I need approval for overtime?

All overtime must be approved in advance by your immediate supervisor. Be sure to record reasons for overtime on your time sheet. Failure to secure approval to work overtime or failure to record overtime hours worked could result in disciplinary action, up to and including termination.

5. How do I keep track of the time I work?

Company time sheets are to be filled out on a daily basis by all hourly and/or nonexempt associates, indicating actual time started, when you leave and return from lunch (or dinner), and actual time work ended for the day. All hours must be entered in decimal form (e.g., 7 hours and 45 minutes = 7.75). Always round to the closest quarter of an hour (for example, 4 hours and 20 minutes = 4.25; 6 hours and 55 minutes = 7.0). At the end of a pay period, total all hours compensated in each of the two weeks of the period and determine any overtime hours to be paid for that week (over 40 hours equals overtime).

Record any vacation, sick, personal, or other paid time to be received. All time records must be turned into your manager by noon on the Monday following the end of a pay period for approval. These are reviewed, approved or corrected and routed to Accounting for payroll processing.

6. When am I paid?

Paychecks are distributed by managers the Friday following the end of a pay period, usually by noon. In no circumstances will checks be issued earlier than Thursday afternoon, and then only with the approval of your manager.

7. When I leave employment with unused vacation or leave, do I receive pay in lieu of time off?

Associates terminated due to resignation, layoff, release, or medical disability are eligible to receive their regular rate of pay for any vacation and personal leave time earned and accrued but not taken by the last official day of work.

b. COMPARABLE WORTH AND PAY EQUITY

One issue you need to be aware of in terms of salary administration is comparable worth or pay equity. Simply, these terms refer to equal pay for equal performance and are closely tied to the issue of job discrimination.

Is a janitor's job worth as much as a secretary's? Is an administrator's job as important to the company as an engineer's? These are tough issues that are not easily addressed.

To help fairly evaluate the worth of jobs, some companies develop systems whereby jobs can be rated based on various criteria determined to be important to the company, for instance: educational requirements, decision-making ability, control, etc. In Canada, pay equity legislation is in the works in several jurisdictions.

Obviously, salary administration is a complex issue and beyond the scope of this book. Suffice it to say that it is an area which you need to give careful consideration and take steps to assure that your pay practices are fair, consistent, and legal.

c. SALARY REVIEWS

Your handbook should cover the issue of salary reviews and explain how pay decisions are made. Typically, these decisions are tied to the evaluation process. Explain how that system will work in a general sense. Avoid stating the process in such specific terms that you commit yourself to statements that you may not wish to adhere to. A statement such as the following would be appropriate:

> An employee will receive a salary review after the first six months of performance and again after one year of performance. Thereafter, salary reviews will occur on an annual basis. Salary reviews are based on an evaluation of performance by the employee's manager and will be reviewed by the company president.

d. EXPENSES

When employees are on company business, how will you handle any expenses they incur? What if an employee needs to purchase some out-of-stock office supplies purchase some out-of-stock office supplies or materials? Expense reimbursement is an issue that many companies face and it is usually handled either through advances or direct reimbursement. You will need to decide how you prefer to deal with this issue in your company. Here's how you might word a statement in your personnel handbook:

> Expenses incurred by an associate on behalf of the company will be reimbursed to the employee if he or she has obtained prior approval to make the expenditure. A request for reimbursement should be submitted to your manager for approval and payment through proper channels. Whenever possible, associates should request a receipt for an expenditure on the company's behalf. Receipts should be attached to the request for reimbursement.

e. USE OF PERSONAL AUTOMOBILES — MILEAGE PER DIEM

The use of personal cars for company business is also an issue that needs to be addressed. Do you have company cars available for employee use on company business? If so, you may want to discourage the use of personal vehicles.

> Personal cars are to be used for company business only when company cars are not available. Special permission must be granted for the use of your own car.

If employees are required to use their own cars, how will they be reimbursed for that use?

> Mileage reimbursement for the authorized use of personal automobiles for the benefit of the company by associates will be paid according to the company policy at that time.

f. WORK HOURS

> The average work week for nonexempt associates is 40 hours. However, the actual hours of work may vary during the month according to the requirements of the department to which an associate is assigned. For purposes of computing overtime pay, the company's work week runs from 12:01 Sunday morning to 12:00 Saturday night.

The above statement is typical of that used in many companies. It's a general statement, but it provides information on the number of hours considered to be a typical week and offers insight into the issue of overtime pay.

In your handbook you may want to be more specific and include a discussion of office hours.

> The office is open from 7:00 a.m. to 5:30 p.m. on weekdays. Associates' hours are normally scheduled eight hours per day, Monday through Friday. From time to time the company may have to alter the schedule to meet the needs of scheduling or for reasons of efficiency. Managers reserve the right to set or change hours of work for people reporting to them.

It's important to include a statement that allows you the option of rescheduling individual hours in any given week at your discretion based on workload, staffing requirements, etc.

If any standard forms are used for keeping track of hours worked by employees, include examples (see Sample #4).

g. BREAKS

Another area of concern to employees is when they will have lunch and work breaks. These guidelines should be indicated in

SAMPLE #4
TIME SHEET

(Please fill in all the information on this top portion.)

Name __Joe_____ Emp# __001____

Department __Human Resources__ Pay Period __1/11-1/24__

FT __X__   PT _____   Hourly __X__   Salaried _____   Non-Exempt __X__

Date	Time In	Time Out	Hours worked / other
S 1/11			
M 1/12	8:00 / 1:00	12:00 / 5:00	8.0
T 1/13	7:00 / 12:00	11:00 / 4:00	8.0
W 1/14	8:00 / 1:30	12:30 / 6:00	9.0
T 1/15	8:00 / sick	12:00	4.0 / 4.0
F 1/16	8:00 / 1:00	12:00 / 5:00	8.0
S 1/17	10:00	12:00	2.0
	WEEK	TOTAL	43.0

Date	Time In	Time Out	Hours worked / other
S 1/18			
M 1/19	Holiday		8.0
T 1/20	8:00 / 2:00	1:00 / 6:00	9.0
W 1/21	9:00 / 1:00	12:00 / 5:00	7.0
T 1/22	8:00 / 1:00	12:00 / 5:00	8.0
F 1/23	8:00 / 1:00 / Dr. appt (personal)	12:00 / 3:00	6.0 / 2.0
S 1/24			
	WEEK	TOTAL	40.0

Date used: Hours

Vacation _____		
Sick _____	1/15	4.0
Personal _____	1/23	2.0
Other __Holiday__	1/19	8.0
REGULAR HOURS _____		66.0
OVERTIME _____		3.0
TOTAL HOURS *		83.0

Overtime explanation:
__Wk 1 - end of year W-2__
_____processing_____

Approved By: _____

* "TOTAL HOURS" = Vacation + Sick + Personal + Other + Regular Hours (actual hours <u>worked</u>) + overtime.

your handbook and may be worded as follows:

> Each full-time associate is entitled to a one-hour lunch break unless other arrangements are made with your manager. Lunch time is not to be used to accrue time off unless authorized by your manager. All food is to be eaten only in the break room or in designated outside areas.

The issue of breaks can become a bit more complex, especially when dealing with workers who may be full time, part time or something between. The following example offers a suggested way of dealing with this issue:

> All full-time associates are allowed to take a maximum 15-minute break during the first half of their scheduled hours and then again during the last half of their work hours. Breaks should be taken in designated areas (break room, picnic table area, etc.). Breaks are considered paid time. They cannot be used to accrue time off or to leave early.
>
> For part-time associates, the following chart will be used as a guide for breaks (paid) and lunches (unpaid):

Working hours	Breaks
0-2 hours	none
2-4½ hours	one 15-minute break
5-6 hours	½ hour lunch and one 15-minute break
6½ hours +	½ hour lunch and two 15-minute breaks

h. ABSENTEEISM

Any company's successful operation depends in large part on the regular attendance of each of its associates. Each job fits into a pattern of production. Obviously, unnecessary or unexcused absences or tardiness affect company operations and place an unfair burden on other employees. A uniform attendance policy helps inform all employees of the importance of adhering to certain guidelines and establishes the basis for disciplinary action should it be necessary.

> The company requires and expects all associates to work according to their normal schedules. It is also important for associates to arrive at their jobs at the appointed time.

You may also want to clearly define certain terms in your handbook so an employee is aware of what constitutes such things as *tardiness*, or *unexcused absences*.

> *Tardiness* is defined as not being at your work station at your scheduled starting time. You should be at your work station ready to begin work at your scheduled starting time, not just arriving at the building at that time. If you have a problem getting to work at your scheduled time due to transportation or family conflicts, you may be able to alter your schedule with your manager's approval. Excessive tardiness will have an adverse effect on consideration for promotions and/or salary increases and may result in other disciplinary actions including termination.
>
> An *excused absence* occurs when you properly notify your manager in advance that you will not be able to work a particular day (or part of a day) and your manager approves your absence. Depending on the situation, you may use accrued sick or personal time to prevent loss of earnings due to an excused absence. Excused absences in excess of the allowed sick and personal time you are entitled to will be handled on a case-by-case basis by your manager

and the Human Resources Manager.

An *unexcused absence* occurs when you are absent and do not properly notify your manager or fail to get approval for the occurrence. You will not be paid for time missed due to unexcused absences and you will also receive a written warning for each occurrence. You are encouraged to discuss any extenuating circumstances with your manager, director, or the Human Resources Manager. An associate who fails to report to work for three consecutive days will be considered to have voluntarily terminated.

Certainly there will be times when even the best of employees will be absent or tardy. In these cases, employees need to know the procedure for notifying the company. A statement such as the following works well:

> If you are going to be absent or more than 30 minutes late to work, telephone your manager as far in advance as possible or at least within a half hour after you are expected to be at work. Asking another associate, friend, or relative to give this notification is not considered proper notification except under emergency conditions or as previously approved by your manager.

If your company is located in an area that receives heavy snow during the winter or sudden floods during the spring or summer, you know that unforeseen circumstances can create difficulties for employees trying to get to work. While you don't want employees risking their lives to get to the office, you do need to establish guidelines so that inclement weather doesn't become an excuse to take a day off. Here's how one company has addressed this problem:

> Inclement conditions that prevent you from reporting to work are conditions over which the company has no control. Therefore:
>
> 1. In fairness to all, only those who report to work during those inclement conditions will be paid. The pay will be equal to the actual hours worked. Anyone who does not report to work will not be paid. You may, however, elect to take vacation or personal time to prevent loss of earnings (full-time associates) or make up the time, with your manager's approval, during the calendar week in which the inclement weather occurred.
>
> 2. If you are allowed to go home early during inclement conditions, you will be paid only for the hours worked.
>
> 3. If all associates are sent home by the company or if we are not able to open, everyone will be paid for all hours they were scheduled to work in that day (maximum of three days).

7
HIRING AND FIRING

We are an equal opportunity employer in all personnel decisions. It is the objective of the company to hire individuals who are qualified for positions or employment by virtue of job-related standards of education, training, and experience and to avoid all unlawful employment and promotion practices.

The above statement is a common — and important — one used in many personnel handbooks. It indicates your commitment to making hiring and other employment decisions on the basis of job-related standards rather than subjective judgments based on such things as race, gender, age, or physical handicap.

Merely making such a statement, of course, is not enough. You must make sure that your hiring procedures reflect a non-discriminatory stance. Avoiding discrimination is no longer only a matter of conscience — it is now a matter of law. Be aware of the anti-discrimination laws in your area and take steps to ensure that your company obeys them.

The specifics of your hiring procedures should also be addressed. Do you have a standard application form? Include a blank one in the handbook. Sample #5 is a common type of application form. None of the questions on your application form should touch on an applicant's race, color, religion, national origin, age, sex, marital status, or disability. Table #1 indicates what the prohibited areas of questioning are.

In addition to the kind of general policy statement discussed above, you should include information on the aspects of your hiring practices that will be of specific interest to your employees, particularly your policies and procedures regarding hiring from within the company.

a. PROMOTING FROM WITHIN

Companies expect loyalty from their employees and, in turn, should signal to employees that they will be loyal to them. One very important way to do this is to establish hiring policies that focus on promoting from within and helping employees to develop their skills.

Hiring from your existing job force often makes good sense. If you have an employee applicant who is minimally qualified for the position, shows potential and the desire to learn, and has been preparing for the possibility of an opening, it's usually a good idea to at least give that employee a chance at the job. Why?

- It's good for the morale of the entire company. People like to see "underdogs" achieve. Promoting from within supports the feeling that "this could happen to me."

- Your training time is minimized. When you hire someone who is already familiar with your company and its policies, procedures, and personnel, you cut drastically into the time it would normally take for a new employee to be "up and running."

If you're uncertain about whether to give an internal candidate the chance at a new position, try to arrange a probationary

SAMPLE #5
APPLICATION FORM

Name: _____

Address: _____

_____

Job applied for: _____ Date: _____

Are you seeking: ☐ Full-time ☐ Part-time ☐ Temporary

Availability? _____ Shift preference _____

EDUCATION OR TRAINING: Please indicate your education and/or training background that is relevant to the job you are applying for:

High school _____

Military service, schools, or training _____

Other training _____

WORK EXPERIENCE: Please list your work experience beginning with your most recent job held. If you were self-employed, give firm name.

Name of employer: _____

Address: _____

Employed from: _____ to _____

Beginning salary: _____ Final salary: _____

Job title: _____

Duties performed: _____

_____

Reason for leaving: _____

_____

[Include space for additional employer information as necessary]

May we contact your present employer?   Yes   No

CERTIFICATION: My signature below certifies that all information in this application is correct and complete to the best of my knowledge and belief and that I understand that intentionally false information could result in refusal of employment or discharge. I also authorize the employers, schools, or persons named above to provide information regarding my employment, education, character, and qualifications.

Signature: _____ Date: _____

TABLE #1
PROHIBITED AREAS OF QUESTIONING IN EMPLOYMENT INTERVIEWS

Subject	Legal	Illegal
Race		You can't ask any question referring to race or color.
Religion or creed		You can't ask any questions about religious denomination or observance of religious holidays.
National origin		You cannot ask any question on lineage or nationality or any question seeking information on the applicant's parents or spouse.
Sex		You cannot ask for any indication of an applicant's sex.
Marital status		You cannot ask whether the applicant is married, divorced, or separated or for any information on the spouse or children.
Family planning		You can't ask about any plans for family — present or future.
Age	You can ask, "Are you between 18 and 70?"	You can't ask, "How old are you?"
Arrest	You can ask if an applicant has ever been convicted of a crime.	You can't ask if an applicant has ever been arrested.
Birthplace		You cannot ask for any information on applicant's birthplace or the birthplace of the applicant's parents or spouse.

TABLE #1 — Continued

Disability	You can ask about any work-related impairment.	You cannot ask, "Have you ever been treated for any of the following?"
Name	You can ask if an applicant has ever worked under another name.	You cannot ask for the maiden name of a married woman.
Photograph		You cannot ask for a photograph before employment.
Citizenship	You may ask, "Are you a citizen of this country?"	You may not ask, "Of what country are you a citizen?" or whether the applicant is a native-born citizen.
Education	You may ask about educational, vocational, or professional schooling.	
Experience	You may ask about work experience.	
Military	You may ask about military service.	You may not ask about military experience in the armed forces of another country.

period. Make the requirements of the position very clear to the new employee and let him or her know that if, after the end of a specific period of time, he or she isn't meeting those requirements, you will refill the position.

The first step you need to take is to examine your hiring procedures. If you don't have clearly outlined procedures for how to fill an open position, employees may be confused and disappointed. Most employees automatically assume that internal applicants will be given preference. If this isn't the case, make sure you communicate it to employees. It will help eliminate problems later.

During the hiring process, you can explain to employees what the chances for advancement within the company are. In some companies there is a requirement that an employee be in a position for at least six months before being allowed to interview for another position. If this is the case with your company, let the new employee know that. Also explain how your hiring process works.

Your employee handbook should clearly outline your internal procedures for dealing with job openings. A typical approach is as follows:

1. A notice announcing each job vacancy will be posted on the bulletin boards in the break room and on each level of the building for a period of five consecutive working days. Interested associates who meet the minimum qualifications may apply for a posted job by notifying the "person to contact" in the department in which the opening has occurred. Associates who have been in their current positions less than six months are ineligible.

2. Associates will be given first consideration as candidates for job vacancies. However, the company does reserve the right to also recruit outside candidates who have the skills or experience needed for the job.

3. The manager in whose department the vacancy occurs will be the person responsible for making the hiring decision. While in-house candidates receive priority consideration for job openings, it is not a guarantee of a new job. All things being equal, the in-house candidate will be offered the position; however, an all cases, the job candidate deemed to be the best qualified will be offered the job.

4. The primary factors taken into account in all promotion and transfer decisions will be the relative ability and merit of all candidates. In reviewing the qualifications of candidates for an open position, the manager or other appointed interviewer will consider each individual's job-related skills, knowledge, experience, ability, efficiency, initiative and attitude; attendance record; past job performance; and, where required, results on tests of job-related skills.

5. The company reserves the right to transfer associates to different positions when it is necessary to maintain efficient operations or production. Associates who are permanently transferred to a lower-paying job may receive a lower rate of pay. These situations will be handled on a case-by-case basis by the associate's manager, director, and the Human Resources Manager.

Make sure that employees are aware that this information is in their handbook by referring to it when new positions come up. For instance:

We have an opening for a clerk typist. Please take a look at your handbook if you have questions about how the hiring process will work.

It's crucial that the procedures are applied fairly and consistently throughout the company. The most important thing to remember when filling any position is that you want to maintain the morale of your existing staff. Showing favoritism, bending the rules for certain employees, or simply ignoring the rules are quick ways to create internal morale problems.

Obviously, no company wants to always promote from within. Sometimes it simply doesn't make sense to fill a position with an internal applicant. When hiring outside the company, you can still signal your loyalty by establishing policies for the rehire of former associates and encouraging internal referrals:

> Associates who terminate voluntarily and are later rehired will be rehired as new associates, no matter how short or long the period of time between termination and rehire.
>
> Associates are encouraged to recommend to the company prospective applicants whom they believe to be qualified for employment. Though many excellent associates have been recommended by present associates, the following practices will be observed:
>
> 1. More than one source for applicants will be used.
>
> 2. The best qualified and most suitable applicant, regardless of the source, will be hired.

b. HIRING RELATIVES

Whatever the size of your organization, the issue of hiring relatives is bound to come up. In anticipation, you should have a clear policy regarding this practice.

If yours is a small, family-owned business, you may already be largely staffed with relatives and this may not be an issue you feel needs to be addressed in your handbook. As your business grows, however, you may want to devote some attention to this issue. Here's how one company addresses the issue of hiring relatives:

> The company may hire relatives of current associates as long as the new associate works in a different department than the current associate. The company will consider an application for employment or a transfer request from an associate's relative as long as it does not create a supervisory relationship between relatives. The company recognizes the sensitive nature of having family members employed by the same company and will take care to avoid difficult situations.
>
> The company may employ relatives for temporary positions even in the same department, provided a clear understanding exists that the employment relationship is strictly temporary and will not necessarily lead to full- or part-time employment. Of course, any relative hired by the company must meet all selection standards and fulfill all job qualifications. The company will not hire a relative in a manager-subordinate relationship under any circumstance.
>
> For purposes of this policy, *relative* means spouse, mother, father, mother-in-law, father-in-law, son, daughter, brother, sister, son-in-law, daughter-in-law, aunt, uncle, and cousin.

c. REDUCTION IN STAFF

Today's turbulent economy means that many companies have had to resort to reductions in staff to get their expenses — and profits — in line. This is never an easy decision and not one that can be implemented simply. As with many other issues of employee management, it pays to have a game plan.

Whether or not you feel that your company will ever have to resort to a reduction in staff, you may want to include a policy statement in your handbook.

> Should conditions necessitate a reduction in our work force, the following steps will be taken:
>
> 1. We will first ask for associates to voluntarily reduce their work hours. This should be discussed with your manager so that you can determine when would be the best time to take time off without pay.
>
> 2. Management may, at any time, decide to only selectively replace vacant positions that exist in the company. We also reserve the right to re-assign the job duties from a vacant position to other associates in the company.
>
> 3. If the actions above fail to provide a significant enough reduction, management will then begin to selectively reduce, either permanently or indefinitely, the current work force.
>
> 4. If all of the above attempts still do not produce acceptable results, we may then have to do an across-the-board reduction in pay and/or hours for all associates. Once the need for a work force reduction has been determined by top management, the directors and managers of the departments to be affected by the layoff will review each of their associate's performance appraisals for the past two years. The director or manager will retain those associates whose appraisals show the best performance. Depending on the extent of the reduction, associates will be retained in descending order according to their performance levels. Associates will be recalled based on a combination of these factors:
>
> (a) The needs of the company
>
> (b) Performance appraisal (the company aims to bring back the best possible associates)
>
> (c) Date of layoff from the company. The Human Resources Manager will make every effort to assist laid-off associates in seeking other employment and in filing for unemployment compensation benefits.

d. VOLUNTARY TERMINATIONS

The employment-at-will principle applies to employees as well as management. An employee can terminate his or her employment at any time, for any reason. Most often this is done when an employee accepts a position with another company.

> A voluntary termination occurs when an associate resigns or is separated from the company at his or her request. If you intend to resign or leave the company voluntarily, it is requested that you give at least two weeks' notice to your immediate supervisor. Notice further in advance of the standard two weeks will be very much appreciated. You may submit your resignation in the form of a letter or on an Employee Resignation Form, which may be obtained from your manager or the Human Resources Manager. As stated in the attendance section, an associate who fails to report to work for three consecutive days will be considered to have voluntarily terminated. No associate will be denied vacation pay or benefits provided herein by failing to give the requested notice.

e. INVOLUNTARY TERMINATIONS

An involuntary termination is a different matter. Employees may be terminated involuntarily when performance does not meet expectations, when rule infractions occur, when reductions in force must be made, etc.

The area of employee termination is a complex one and open to many potential hazards. It is beyond the scope of this book to discuss the issue at length. Suffice it to say that your handbook should address the issue in some manner. A simple statement, such as the following, will work well:

> Involuntary termination is a separation from employment that occurs without request by the associate. Involuntary terminations include, but are not limited to layoffs, release discharges, and medical disability terminations.

f. EXIT INTERVIEWS

Whether an employee leaves voluntarily or involuntarily, a great deal can be gained by conducting an exit interview. An exit interview is a tool used by many companies to monitor and examine turnover. It can provide you with good information on how you can do things differently with your current and your new employees. There are two functions to an exit interview:

(a) To "process" the terminated employee in an orderly way (You will need to take care of such items as severance pay, insurance premiums, pensions, references, etc.)

(b) To collect information on the employee's reasons for leaving in the case of a voluntary termination

However you choose to handle the exit interview, if you decide that it will be of value to your organization, inform employees of the process in your handbook.

Every associate who leaves the company for any reason will have the opportunity for two separate exit interviews — first with his or her manager and then with the Human Resources Manager. Except under extraordinary circumstances, exit interviews will be conducted on an associate's last day of employment.

g. REFERENCES

References can be a tricky business, providing some legal pitfalls to unwary employers. Courts have ruled in favor of former employees who claim they have been defamed through a bad job reference. An employer can be held accountable to prove anything he or she says about former employees. Providing negative references for former employees can be a dangerous (and expensive) proposition.

But don't immediately assume that the best posture is a silent posture. Employers have also been taken to court for *not* providing pertinent information about a former employee!

There are three key ways to protect yourself when giving references:

(a) Provide references in good faith without malice and provide only factual, job-related information.

(b) Limit the information you provide and the persons authorized to provide that information.

(c) Provide information only to authorized persons and only in an appropriate manner (not over drinks with a crony at the local watering spot or during a round of golf at the club).

Your personnel procedures should be designed to help you avoid — not win — lawsuits. Require that statements be provided in writing to avoid any disputes or misunderstandings about what was said or what was asked. Make this a policy for your company that is followed religiously.

Require that statements made be based only on actual performance issues that can be clearly documented. Have a policy that only a particular department or individual can give references for employees.

When an associate is terminated by resignation, layoff, release, or end of temporary employment, the Human Resources Manager will provide letters of reference, if requested, to help the associate obtain future employment.

All inquiries from prospective employers about a past associate's employment record, performance, or attendance must be referred to the Human Resources Manager. No one else is authorized to release information about a former associate. Any unauthorized releases of information may result in disciplinary action, up to and including discharge, as this may jeopardize the former associate's right to privacy and may subject the company to legal action.

Before the Human Resources Manager will release any information, the former associate must grant consent in writing. Except where specifically requested by the former associate, only information pertaining to dates of employment and final salary will be released. Information regarding character, performance, attendance, ability, personal characteristics, etc. will only be released in response to the former associate's written request.

8
BENEFITS

Why offer benefits to employees? To keep up with the Joneses. And the IBMs. And the corner grocery. Due to the competitive nature of hiring qualified employees, more and more companies are finding that they must offer attractive benefit packages to retain the best workers.

In the early twentieth century, few companies offered any benefits to employees. In the 1940s and 1950s, this began to change and, in the last 20 years, we've seen a preponderance of new benefits, new benefit plans, and growing numbers of companies offering benefits to their employees. Some benefits, such as holidays, minimum vacation time, and worker's compensation coverage, are legislated in some areas of North America. Be sure to check the laws in your area to determine what benefits you must offer your employees.

Benefits can fall into a number of areas including social programs (social security, worker's compensation), insurance and retirement benefits (health, life, etc.), payment for time not worked (vacation, sick time), extra cash payments to employees (educational allowances, suggestion awards), and services (recreational programs, free parking, day care centers, etc.)

The average payment for employee benefit expenses is approximately 37.7% of payroll according to a study by the Chamber of Commerce of the United States. The breakdown is as follows:

9.5%   Social insurance programs

4.2%   Payments to private pension plans

8.6%   Payments to insurance plans

15.4%   All other types of benefits

The study also indicates that there is a large variation among companies, from a low of 20% of payroll for employee benefits to a high of 60%.

Your personnel manual should outline all the benefits available to employees and refer employees to other sources (such as an insurance program booklet) for more information if needed.

For more on employee benefit programs, see *Motivating Today's Work Force*, another title in the Self-Counsel Series.

a. FLEXIBLE BENEFIT PROGRAMS

The work force of the nineties is very diverse and employers are taking steps in many areas to recognize and respond to this diversity. One way to accommodate it is through flexible benefit or "cafeteria" plans.

People work for a variety of reasons and what acts as a motivator for one employee will not necessarily serve the same purpose for another. Cafeteria plans are designed to accommodate the varied needs of today's work force. Employers benefit as well through tax savings. More and more companies are turning to flexible benefit plans as a way of offering employees variety and the opportunity to cater to their personal needs.

This type of plan is often set up using a system of credits or "flexible compensation dollars." Employees receive a certain number of credits or "flexdollars" to spend on the benefits they want. A flexible plan allows employees to sacrifice some of one benefit in order to gain more of another.

If you offer this kind of flexible benefit plan, you will need to outline carefully in your manual how credits are earned or assigned and what options employees have for spending them. Here is how one personnel manual covered this area:

> The company's flexible benefit plan covers the following benefit areas: medical, dental, optional disability, vacation, life insurance, and reimbursement accounts for health care and dependent care. Each benefit area has a core plan. The core plan provides a basic level of coverage that the company feels each employee should have. The flexible plan allows you to supplement your core coverage in the areas of most interest to you. If you want more than core coverage in any benefit area, you must pay for it with flexdollars.
>
> There are two kinds of flexdollars: benefit flexdollars and pay conversion flexdollars. Benefit flexdollars are credits that the company gives you to spend on benefits. Each year the company sets the amount of benefit flexdollars that each type of employee will receive and a core level of benefits in certain benefit areas. The company pays for the core plan in those areas. You can use your benefit flexdollars to pay the difference between the cost of core benefits and any additional benefits you want in any benefit area. Each year, you will choose a benefit package that will best meet your needs. If you choose a benefit package that costs more than the credits the company gives you, you can pay for the extra benefits by converting some of your pay into flexdollars. These pay conversion flexdollars will be deducted on a pre-tax basis from your paychecks throughout the year.

Both employees and the company can benefit through a pay conversion plan such as that outlined above. Pay conversion flexdollars offer a significant advantage over after-tax payroll deductions. They reduce taxable income and current income tax liability because they are deducted from pay before taxes are computed. (Although note that in Canada, most employee benefits are now taxable, so tax advantages will be minimal, if they exist at all.)

b. VACATION

> It is the company's policy to grant vacation time with pay to our full-time associates in order to provide a period of rest and recreation in recognition of services performed. We also grant vacation pay (as opposed to time off) to our part-time associates.

Your handbook should include specific statements about the conditions of vacation and time-off benefits. How much time off is allowed? When is the employee eligible for these benefits? How do benefits vary based on job classifications?

It is traditional for vacation time to increase with length of employment. If that is the case in your company, outline how this time will be earned and when vacation time increases.

> A full-time associate's vacation time will be calculated on length of time in service prior to the last day of the last full pay period in any calendar year. This excludes new associates who have not yet completed 6 months' employment. The following chart outlines paid vacation time earned in relation to length of employment.

After 1 full calendar year   10 days

After 4 full calendar years   15 days

After 8 full calendar years   20 days

Vacation accrues at the rate of 3.08 hours per full pay period worked. Upon completion of six months' employment, new associates will be able to use the vacation hours they accumulated from their date of hire to the 6-month anniversary date. This will equal approximately 40 hours for an associate working 40 hours/week. In January of the following year, the associate will receive the vacation hours accrued from the 6-month anniversary date through the last full pay period in December. In January of the following year, the associate receives a full 2 weeks of vacation.

The following examples illustrate how a system like the one outlined above might work:

(a) An employee begins on February 1, 1995. On August 1, 1995, the employee has accrued and is eligible to use approximately 40.04 hours of vacation (13 pay periods x 3.08 hours = 40.04 hours). On January 1, 1996, the employee has accrued and is eligible to use another 33.88 hours (11 pay periods from August through December x 3.08 hours = 33.88 hours). On January 1, 1997, that employee will receive 80.08 hours of vacation earned during the calendar year 1996.

(b) An employee begins on August 1, 1995. On February 1, 1996, that employee has accrued and is eligible to use approximately 40.04 hours of vacation (13 pay periods x 3.08 hours = 40.04 hours). On January 1, 1997, the employee has accrued and is eligible to use another 73.92 hours (24 pay periods from February through December x 3.08 hours = 73.92 hours). On January 1, 1998, the employee will receive 80.08 hours of vacation earned during the calendar year 1997.

Vacation pay for part-time associates may be calculated differently. Outline in your handbook how this system works.

Vacation pay, as opposed to vacation days, will be paid to part-time associates based on hours worked as of the last day of the last pay period of the calendar year. Vacation pay is calculated as follows: Total hours worked during year, divided by 52 weeks, times rate of pay equals 1 week of vacation pay.

The following chart outlines vacation pay earned in relation to length of employment:

After 1 full calendar year   1 week

After 4 full calendar years   2 weeks

After 8 full calendar years   4 weeks

With the exception of associations who have not completed six months' employment, vacation pay will be paid on the paycheck following the regular payroll run closest to January 1 each year. Associates who have not completed six months' employment by the last day of the last pay period of the calendar year will receive vacation pay following the payroll run closest to July 1 (calculated on hours worked during the previous calendar year from the date of hire through the last pay period in December).

Another important issue you will want to address is that of scheduling vacation time. While it may be obvious to you that employees must request vacation or other time-off benefits in advance, by stating this clearly in your handbook you can avoid problems later. Your handbook should include guidelines that you intend to follow.

You should not, however, promise to assign vacation based on seniority or on a first-come, first-served basis in all cases. Business conditions or other factors may make this impractical at times and you will want to reserve your right to schedule vacations and change vacation schedules as necessary.

> When scheduling a vacation, notify your manager of the dates you would like to take off and get his or her approval well in advance. If you want to take off more than two days in a row, it is strongly suggested that you ask your manager at least ten working days in advance so that arrangements can be made to cover your work. An approval for any vacation time requested will depend on the staffing needs and work load of your department. Scheduling of conflicting vacation requests will be handled on a date-requested basis.

What happens when employees fail to use their allocation of vacation benefits during the specified time (usually one year)? You will need to make decisions on whether employees can carry over that time into the following year. In addition, you will want to specify how much time can be carried over. You may also want to address whether or not employees may be paid cash value for time not used.

> In any calendar year, you can carry over up to one week (forty hours) of vacation time into the next calendar year. However, we strongly encourage you to take all of your vacation time during the year, as you have earned it and deserve a break from work. Vacation time left in excess of forty hours at the end of a calendar year will be lost to you.

c. HOLIDAYS

In the United States, most companies close their offices for certain holidays and pay employees for those days as though they had been worked. Typically, the following days are offered:

New Year's Day
Martin Luther King Day
Presidents' Day
Memorial Day
Independence Day
Labor Day
Veterans' Day
Thanksgiving Day
Christmas Day

In Canada, certain days are legislated general holidays in most provinces. These include:

New Year's Day
Good Friday
Victoria Day
Canada Day
Labour Day
Thanksgiving Day
Remembrance Day
Christmas Day

Some provinces also include a provincial holiday, for example, British Columbia Day in British Columbia.

You may decide to include additional days. For example, you may decide to give the Friday after Thanksgiving (in the United States) or Easter Monday. The choices are yours. Simply indicate clearly in your handbook which days are considered paid holidays.

What happens when one of these holidays occurs on a weekend? Will an employee still be paid for that time? Many companies deal with this issue as follows:

> All full-time associates will receive holiday pay for these days. Company holidays that fall on a Saturday will be observed the preceding Friday. Those that fall on a Sunday will be observed the following Monday.

You will also have to decide what happens if an employee is asked to and agrees to work on a holiday. Will overtime apply where the employee receives one-and-a-half, two, or even three times the regular pay?

d. SICK LEAVE

The issue of sick leave is another critical one which you will want to address in some fashion in your handbook. There are a number of different ways of dealing with the sick leave issue. Some companies do not offer paid time off for sick leave at all, requiring employees to use vacation time for this purpose. Others combine sick, vacation, and personal time into one category that employees can use for any reason. Others offer a certain number of sick days each year and then pay employees a certain percentage of cash value for those days not used. Following is a traditional statement dealing with the issue of sick leave:

> Every full-time associate earns 1.85 hours of paid sick time for every pay period worked during the course of full-time employment at the company, beginning with the date of hire. This is an annual total of 6 days (48 hours for an associate regularly scheduled to work 40 hours/week). You are immediately eligible to use sick time you have earned. If you are ill, inform your manager no later than one-half hour after your scheduled starting time (earlier if possible). It is expected that any sick days taken will be for legitimate reasons.

Just as with vacation time, you will want to deal with the issue of sick leave accrual. Will employees be able to carry over days they have not used? How many days can they accrue?

> Sick time will continue to accrue during your full-time employment to a maximum of 60 days (480 hours for an associate regularly scheduled to work 40 hours/week). An illness of over 1 week in duration will require a signed statement from your physician.

e. PERSONAL LEAVE

When families have children and both parents work, the issue of time off to care for sick family members is an important one. If an employee's child is ill, can the employee use his or her sick time to care for the child or must vacation time be used? One method of dealing with this is the establishment of personal leave, time that employees can use as they wish.

> In addition to regularly scheduled holidays, all full-time associates earn personal time during the course of their employment that can be used at their discretion. Personal time accrues at the rate of .81 hours per pay period. This is an annual total of a little over 2½ days (21 hours). You are immediately eligible to use personal time you have earned. You will need the approval of your manager before taking personal time off. We suggest that you use these hours for attending to personal business, making dental or doctor appointments, and taking extra time off around holidays.

f. PARENTAL/MEDICAL LEAVE

An issue that has come to the forefront today is that of family or parental leave. Both men and women today want to spend time at home after the birth of a child. Maternity, paternity, and/or parental leaves are now law in some areas, so you should first be familiar with the legislation in your area. In the United States, federal legislation concerning family leave is effective as of August, 1993. This law applies to companies with 50 or more employees and requires them to provide leaves of absence for family or medical purposes. Family leaves include leaves for birth or adoption; medical leaves involve illness of employee or employee's child or dependent parent.

In your company manual, lay out the rules for taking leave and also mention any parental leave the company offers beyond the legal minimum.

Medical leave for extended illness or when employees need to care for an ailing relative is another subject that is being closely considered by legislators, so make sure you are up to date on the law for your area.

Following is a typical statement on parental/medical leave that might appear in your handbook:

> All family and medical leave shall be granted in accordance with (state or provincial) and federal laws. Associates (male or female) who have worked for the company for 1 year and who have worked at least 1,000 hours during that year qualify for benefits under this policy. There are two forms of leave:
>
> 1. Family leave. Qualified associates will be permitted to take a leave of up to 6 weeks in a 12-month period for the birth or adoption of a child. Such leave must begin within 16 weeks of the child's birth or adoption.
>
> 2. Medical leave. Each eligible associate is permitted to take up to 2 weeks of medical leave over a 12-month period for his or her own serious illness. Eligible associates are also permitted to take a leave of up to 2 weeks in a 12-month period for the care of a seriously ill spouse, parent, or child. The company reserves the right to request verification from a health care provider to establish the need for leave involving a serious illness.
>
> Family/medical leave is unpaid; however, the company will provide group insurance benefits for associates during family or medical leave under the same conditions that existed before the leave was taken, and time-off benefits will continue to accrue during the leave. Associates requesting family or medical leave are asked to notify their manager as far in advance of the desired leave as possible.

g. OTHER TIME OFF

In addition to time off for vacation, holidays, and the leaves described above, there are other instances when employees may be away from work. Consider carefully the policies you want to develop for things such as jury duty, military leave, funeral leave, doctor and dental appointments, etc. In addition, be sure to check local law affecting employees' rights in these areas. The examples below show typical wording regarding policies on these issues.

1. Jury duty

> When you are required to serve as a juror, the company will pay you the difference between your salary for your regularly scheduled hours and the amount you receive for jury duty. In the event you are subpoenaed to appear in court, you will be released from normal duties with pay for a period of time not to exceed eight hours total. Paid time off will be granted only for the time that it takes to present testimony and not merely to act as an observer to legal proceedings. No allowance of pay will be made if you are summoned to court as a result of your personal involvement as a litigant.

2. Military leave

> Summer encampments for the National Guard or Reserves duty or other types of military leave will be taken off without pay. You do not

have to use vacation or personal time unless you want to. This time off from work will generally not affect your benefits or vacation, sick or personal time accruals (depending on the amount of time away from the job). Please notify your manager as far in advance as possible of the dates you will be gone so that arrangements can be made to cover your work during that time. The company will grant all military leaves of absence in accordance with the laws of _____. Please see the Human Resources Manager for details.

3. Funeral leave

We will grant all full-time associates reasonable bereavement time off without loss of pay. In case of a death in your immediate family, you can take a maximum of five days off with pay for the emergency period. Members of the immediate family are considered to be your spouse, children, father, mother, brothers, sisters, grandparents, grandchildren, father-in-law or mother-in-law. For absences due to the death of a relative other than a member of your immediate family, you will be allowed a maximum of eight hours funeral leave with pay. Funeral leave days are non-cumulative from one year to the next and may only be used for funeral leave.

4. Doctor and dental appointments

You are encouraged to make doctor and dental appointments during lunch hours or near the beginning or the end of your work day. Appointments that require you to be away from work can be taken as either personal or sick time or unpaid time off. Always check with your manager in advance when making appointments.

5. Elections

If you are eligible to vote in any general election, you may request time off for voting. Time off must be for the purpose of voting and taken during the forenoon. Time off will be given without loss of pay.

6. General leaves of absence

There may be occasions when employees request a leave of absence that is not related to the birth or adoption of a child or to a medical need. An employee may feel "burned out," may want the opportunity to spend some time at home, to take a break from the corporate world, etc. Will you grant this type of leave? If so, you may wish to use a statement such as the following:

> On occasion, it may be necessary for an associate to be absent from work for an extended period of time for reasons other than a disability, family, or medical leave. General leaves of absence will be permitted depending on the reasons and circumstances prompting such a request. The request must be submitted in writing to your manager and should be supported by valid reasons. It then must be approved by your division director. General leaves of absence are taken without pay. General leaves may be granted for a minimum of one month and a maximum of three months. When returning from leave, the associate will be reinstated to his or her former position or a similar other position which may be available, at the appropriate rate of pay.

h. AFFECT OF LEAVES OF ABSENCE ON BENEFITS

You will need to address the question of how leaves will affect an employee's other benefits. Will the time off be included or excluded when calculating the various benefits? What if the employee does not return to work after the leave of absence?

> The company will provide group insurance benefits for associates under the same conditions that existed before the leave was taken for up to one month. Leaves beyond one month will require that the associate pay the full premium for any insurance benefits. Time-off benefits (vacation, sick, personal time) will continue to accrue during a leave of absence (less than three months), provided that the associate does return to work after the leave period has ended. These periods will not affect the timing of performance and salary reviews, nor will they affect anniversary dates.
>
> Salary reviews that may occur during a leave of any kind will not be conducted until an associate returns to work. Time off requests for less than one month will be treated as a departmental scheduling concern and will be at the discretion of your manager. All vacation, personal or sick time available to you should be used first, depending on the circumstances of your request. Additional time off approved beyond this will be without pay. Holidays occurring during a leave of absence will be unpaid.

i. INSURANCE

Your employee handbook should not attempt to describe in great detail the benefits available to employees under your employee health and other paid benefit plans. Instead, briefly refer to the different plans available and direct employees to the plan itself, the plan summary, or the personnel administrator for further details. Being too specific about benefits could result in your being unclear or misleading and expose your company to liability.

In addition to the general material you include in your handbook, therefore, you might want to include a statement like this:

> If this handbook inadvertently says anything that disagrees with the formal documents, the formal documents are the ones that will control.

When outlining the general characteristics of each plan, consider what information employees are likely to be interested in. Explain the options available, the cost to the employee (if any), the availability of additional options to be paid by the employee, eligibility requirements, and sign-up procedures.

1. Health insurance "buy back"

With the preponderance of two-paycheck families in today's society, it is not unlikely for an employee to have insurance both through his or her own company and through the company where his or her spouse works. This double coverage is expensive to companies who must pay premiums for unnecessary insurance. To overcome this problem, some companies offer what are called *buy-back plans*. These plans offer incentives for employees to waive health coverage through the company where they work when they are already covered under a spouse's plan. Following is how such a policy statement might read.

> Some of our associates will be covered by their spouse's or other family member's health insurance, and will therefore not need to sign up for the coverage the company offers. To ensure that we don't double up on health insurance coverage on our associates, we offer an annual bonus of $200 for every associate who is eligible but does not take our health

insurance for an entire plan year. This bonus is paid on the first regular paycheck after the beginning of the plan year. This amount is prorated if you cancel coverages during the year, or if you are a new associate and don't need the coverage and have completed six months of employment.

By encouraging our employees to have coverage under only one health policy, we are making an effort to help control the overall cost of health insurance.

2. Disability coverage

Disability programs are designed to provide employees with a source of income during times when they are medically unable to work due to non-work-related illnesses or injuries (work-related illnesses or injuries are covered under worker's compensation plans). Companies typically offer both short-term and long-term disability coverage.

Short-term disabilities are defined as a non-work-related illness or injury that medically prevents an employee from doing his or her job for up to three months. Following is an example of the type of language you might use to discuss your short-term disability benefits:

> All full-time associates are covered by our short-term disability income plan beginning the first of the month following one full calendar month of employment. There is no cost to you for this plan. There is a two-week waiting period before this benefit will actually begin. You may use any accrued sick, personal, or vacation time available to you to offset this without-pay waiting period.
>
> Upon completing the waiting period, you will receive the short-term disability benefit of two-thirds of your regular weekly pay (does not include overtime, bonuses, holidays, etc.), for up to three months after the first day you can't work. You may combine any paid sick, vacation, or personal leave you have available with your disability pay; however, when combined, the amount may not exceed your regular pay.

As an example of how this system might work, suppose an employee falls down the stairs and is injured to the extent that he or she cannot come to work. This happens on July 15, 1995. On July 29, the two-week waiting period has been satisfied and the employee begins receiving benefits of two-thirds of his or her regular pay. These benefits would then continue as long as the employee's doctor says the employee can't work, up until October 15, 1995. At that point, if the employee still can't work, the long-term disability portion of the plan would begin. Typically long-term disability is not paid by the company. In order for the employee to begin receiving this benefit for an extended health problem, he or she would have to have been a subscriber to the plan.

Your statement on short-term disability can also indicate how pay is calculated and how checks will be issued. You will also want to indicate the deductions that will be made from these checks.

> Short-term disability income is prorated to one-fifth for each work week day of the disability. Checks will be issued through our regular payroll system on a bi-weekly basis. All statutory deductions will be withheld (social security, federal and state or provincial withholdings), as well as all regular payroll deductions for any other contributory benefits to which you may subscribe.

You may also want to go into the process involved when applying for short-term disability.

> If you become disabled and cannot report to work for more than the two-week waiting period, contact the Human Resources Manager as soon as possible. You and your physician will have to fill out forms to verify your disability and qualify you for this benefit. Every four weeks, a doctor's statement verifying continued disability must be submitted to the Human Resources Manager in order to continue your short-term disability income.
>
> The continuation of your short-term disability income presumes that you do not engage in any other work for remuneration or profit. It also presumes that the company has reason to believe that you will return to work after your short-term disability ends. We retain the right to discontinue or reduce benefits if either of the above conditions are not met. All accruals for vacation, sick, and personal time will continue for the total three months of a short-term disability. There are many more details to this plan than can be outlined here. Please see the Human Resources Manager for more details.

Another important consideration when dealing with short-term disability issues is the status of the job being vacated, even for a brief period of time. How long will you leave the position vacant before filling it? What guarantees will you offer employees that their job will be available when they return? You may wish to consider including a statement such as the following:

> Every reasonable effort will be made to keep your position open until you can return to work from a short-term disability. This includes redistribution of work to other associates and hiring temporary replacements if necessary. There may be some situations, however, where this would not be practical, and we therefore reserve the right to fill a position if it becomes necessary. Disabilities of longer than three months will have to be evaluated on a case-by-case basis when it comes to keeping your job open. If we feel we must hire someone for your position, every effort will be made to place you in another suitable position should one become available when you are able to return to work.

Long-term disabilities can be defined as non-work-related illnesses or injury that medically prevent an employee from doing his or her job beyond a period of three months (the short-term disability period). Long-term disability is generally offered through the company; however, premiums are typically paid by the employee who can choose the level of coverage desired. In your handbook, you can use wording similar to that given in the examples above on short-term disability.

3. Extended benefits after leaving company

What happens to an employee's benefits when he or she leaves the company? This is a common question that employees will have and one that should be addressed in the handbook. The following statement is an example of the type of language you may want to use.

> If your employment with the company ends due to resignation, voluntary or involuntary termination or layoff, certain benefits can be converted to individual coverage. (Go on to outline what those benefits are in accordance with the plans offered.)

U.S. federal law permits certain persons who lose their coverage under the employer's group medical insurance plan to continue under the plan for a specified period of time, subject to the payment of premiums by the employee.

Employees are typically permitted to continue group medical coverage when insurance is terminated due to reduction of work hours or termination of employment, other than termination due to gross misconduct. An employee's spouse and dependent children are also permitted to continue when eligibility for coverage is lost as a result of divorce or legal separation, loss of dependent child status due to age or marriage, or the associate's death, termination of employment, or reduction of work hours.

Employees are not, however, eligible for continuance if they have other group medical coverage in existence (unless the coverage does not include pre-existing conditions) or they are covered by Medicare.

Coverage typically continues until:

(a) the end of the period of continuance to which she or she is entitled;

(b) the date the group plan terminates;

(c) if the person stops paying premiums, the end of the period for which premium payment was last made;

(d) the date the person becomes covered under another group medical plan (unless the other group plan does not cover pre-existing conditions); or

(e) the date the person becomes entitled to Medicare.

Employees should be informed of the process through which they are able to continue with insurance coverage:

> In the event of a divorce or legal separation, or a dependent child's ceasing to be a qualified dependent by reason of age or marriage, the covered associate and/or his or her dependents must notify the employer within 60 days of the qualifying event. Within 14 days of such notice to the company or within 14 days of your date of termination, the company will provide the employee and/or dependents with a form to elect continued coverage. The company is under the same obligation to provide a continuation option form in the event of an employee's death or termination of employment or reduction of work hours. The continuation option form provides detailed information to associates and their dependents on the procedures to follow to elect continued coverage.

j. SHARING OF COMPANY PROFITS

Does your company offer a profit-sharing plan? If so, you will want to include information on the plan and how it works. Which employees are eligible? When are distributions made? What do the distributions consist of? What will determine whether or not a distribution is made during a given time period?

Profit-sharing plans are a good way to tie employee performance to company results — with benefits directly tied to those results.

> A plan for sharing company profits has been developed by the company to formally recognize the continuing contributions associates have made toward the future of the company. All employees who were employed by the company on the last day of the fiscal year (December 31) and who are employed on the date the sharing of profits checks are

distributed (February 1) are eligible to receive a distribution of benefits.

The company will distribute 10% of any profits each year to all eligible associates. "Profits" will be determined as of the end of the fiscal year and the actual distribution of checks to associates will be made on February 1.

This 10% of profits will be distributed to each eligible associate in the same proportion as that eligible associate's salary is to the total salary for the fiscal year.

k. WORKER'S COMPENSATION

Worker's compensation coverage is compulsory for most businesses in North America. You do not need to go into great detail in your personnel manual about the program as that information is too complex to include in its entirety and is available elsewhere. What you should do is mention that the company has coverage, how to report an accident, and where employees can find more information.

The company carries worker's compensation insurance. In accordance with the laws of the State/Province of ____, the company will pay benefits arising out of illness or injury incurred in the course of employment. If an associate has an accident while at work, regardless of how trivial it might seem, the associate must report it to his or her supervisor. The supervisor will report it to the appropriate personnel and authorities. This is for our employees' protection and to comply with legal requirements. For more information on the Worker's Compensation program, see ——-.

l. UNEMPLOYMENT COMPENSATION

Outline briefly your company's involvement with government unemployment compensation programs. Again, details are unnecessary as the information is readily available elsewhere.

United States —

The company is required to pay a tax to both federal and state governments based on its payroll. This tax is applied to an unemployment insurance account. These monies are disbursed by the state to unemployed persons who are eligible for benefits.

Canada —

The company is required to deduct unemployment insurance premiums from employees' pay and to pay company premiums according to government regulations. These premiums support the unemployment insurance program across the country. Benefits are available to unemployed workers who qualify. For more information, contact the U.I.C. office in your area.

m. EMPLOYEE EDUCATION

Many companies offer educational opportunities to employees to allow them to improve the skills required to perform their current job as well as to help them develop skills that might be appropriate for future jobs. In your handbook, you will want to address what types of educational opportunities you will support, how they will be paid for (for instance, you may choose to use a reimbursement plan rather than paying up-front costs), and how employees can request educational benefits. Include examples of any forms used in this process, such as the education request form shown in Sample #6.

The company encourages its associates to take advantage of continuing education opportunities. If you are interested in attending a seminar or class that is directly related to your job, talk to your manager. He or she will decide if the course is appropriate and the cost is justified in regard to the budget available. For an approved one- to five-day course, payment will be made by the company in advance. Reasonable travel and accommodation expenses will also be paid for. For a course that covers more than five days, an employee will be reimbursed for tuition and materials needed when evidence of satisfactory completion is submitted.

Some companies require that employees report back on what they learned from the training. This is a good way to emphasize the need for employees to obtain something of value from the courses they attend, to apply that value to their jobs, and to provide the company with information on the merit of various courses and seminars. Sample #7 shows an education evaluation form.

> Every associate who attends a seminar or class is expected to prepare a written report or fill out a Training Evaluation Form within 30 days explaining what was learned and how it will benefit the company. This report should be submitted to your manager. Failure to do so may result in restricting future attendance at other seminars and classes.

n. EMPLOYEE-ASSISTANCE PROGRAMS

Employee-assistance programs (EAPs) are a way to help identify and solve concerns in the lives of your employees. Family and marriage problems, stress and depression, alcohol and drug abuse, and legal, financial, career, and health issues are addressed through these plans. These types of problems have been estimated to affect 10% to 25% of the work force at any given time.

Any work force constitutes a group of people bringing with them to the job diverse needs, skills — and personal problems. These problems can be costly to an organization. Researchers have estimated that alcoholic employees, for instance, can cost a company an extra $1,000 per year. Other estimates give a figure of 25% of the employee's base salary.

Some invisible costs include accidents, increased absenteeism, tardiness, loss of morale among workers, impaired judgment, and impaired ability to make decisions.

EAPs offer confidential help and provide time for employees to "straighten out." Although programs differ in many respects, they also share some characteristics:

- Many are accessible not only to employees but also to their families
- Many offer free or partially paid-for counseling
- Most programs offer services that range from 24-hour hotlines to in-person diagnostic and referral services. Others offer, in addition, counseling and treatment.

When a company begins to consider the establishment of an EAP two questions must be answered:

(a) What is the cost/benefit ratio? Can an organization expect a reasonable return for its investment of resources in an employee-assistance program?

(b) What is the level of cost effectiveness? Can an occupational alcoholism program be conducted at acceptable effectiveness levels in terms of optimum return per dollar invested?

Most employers have found the answer to both of these questions to be yes. Employee-assistance programs can benefit not only the troubled employee, but the employer as well. Both the cost-effectiveness of these programs and the outstanding results demonstrated among troubled employees make EAPs an outlet that more and more companies are looking into.

Here is a statement included in the employee handbook of a company that offers an employee-assistance program:

> The company provides assistance to employees in need of counseling for personal or emotional problems through an Employee-Assistance Program. The program we sponsor is a counseling and informational service designed to help make our work environment better for all concerned. The goal of the EAP is to help individuals cope with problems or concerns before health, family life, or job performance is affected. The program offers sensitive, professional, and confidential support.
>
> This is a free service for you and your family members. The company pays for this benefit because we care, and we know that anyone can have personal problems from time to time. When these problems are resolved, people perform better on their jobs.
>
> The EAP phone lines are answered 24 hours a day. The numbers to call are __. Simply make an appointment with a counselor. Counseling over the phone is available, though in-person sessions are preferable. Family members are also encouraged to use the EAP. The EAP counselor can work with you to assess your situation. With a little help, most people begin to resolve their problems.
>
> Short-term counseling is provided and other helpful community resources are suggested if necessary. If a referral is made, they will follow up with you to see if the help you received was satisfactory. Payment for any services outside the Employee-Assistance Program is your responsibility. The EAP counselor will work with you to find the best, most affordable care available. They are aware of many free services in the area, and many programs that are covered by insurance benefits.

SAMPLE #6
EDUCATION REQUEST FORM

EDUCATION REQUEST FORM

Seminars, workshops, short courses

Name _____ Date _____

Position _____ Dept. _____

Program title _____

Sponsor _____ Fee _____

Location _____ Dates _____

Stated course objectives (attach brochure) _____
_____

Explain reason for attending and how course relates to your job _____
_____

Itemized estimate of additional expenses _____
_____

Employee signature _____ Date _____
(Read instructions on back before signing)

Manager ❑ Approved ❑ Not approved

Reasons _____
_____

Signature _____ Date _____

Director ❑ Approved ❑ Not approved

Reasons _____
_____

Signature _____ Date _____

Human Resources comments _____
_____

Signature _____ Date _____

Total expenses _____ Date reimbursed _____

Date evaluation returned _____

SAMPLE #6 — Continued

INSTRUCTIONS

Use this form when requesting approval to attend a seminar, workshop, or short course (generally less than 5 days in length) at company expense and on company time.

Before attending:

1. Fill out this form completely at least one month prior to the start of the seminar, workshop, or short course. Be sure to get estimates on expenses.
2. Obtain approvals from your manager and director. If your request is not approved, your manager will discuss the reasons with you. You will receive a training evaluation form when notified of approval.
3. When your request is approved, have your manager request a check for payment of your registration fee.
4. Contact the travel department for travel and accommodation arrangements if needed.

After course completion:

1. Complete training evaluation form. Return it and discuss with your manager within two weeks.
2. Submit a completed expense report (with receipts attached) to your manager. He or she will review and approve for payment and forward to the accounting department. You will be reimbursed within reasonable processing time.

Agreement between employee and company:

Your signature on this application form attests to your understanding that:

1. You will complete all evaluation and reporting functions required by this program.
2. Participation in this course is voluntary and is neither a condition of employment nor a guarantee of advancement.
3. The company reserves the right to amend, modify, or discontinue the employee education and development program at any time.

SAMPLE #7
EDUCATION EVALUATION FORM

OUTSIDE TRAINING/EDUCATION PROGRAM EVALUATION

This form has been designed to help evaluate training/education programs conducted by outside organizations. Your comments will be of great value in determining future participation in this and other similar programs. Please return the completed form and other requested information to your manager within two weeks after you return from the program.

Name _____

Job title _____ Department _____

Title of program _____

Sponsoring organization/institution _____

Length of program _____

Dates attended _____ Tuition _____

1. The program's objectives were stated as follows:

   _____

   Objectives were: ❑ on target ❑ sometimes on target ❑ not met

2. Based on your needs, the level of the course was:

   ❑ about right ❑ too elementary ❑ too advanced

3. Compared to yours, the job level of other participants was:

   ❑ about the same ❑ mostly below ❑ mostly above

   (Please attach a list of participants, including name, company, and job title. If a list is not available, write down the names of people you talked with at the program, their titles, and companies.)

4. Organization of the course content was:

   ❑ good ❑ fair ❑ poor

5. Were you given an outline of the course? ❑ yes ❑ no

   (Please attach either a class schedule or an outline for the course. Include the time spent on each subject.)

6. Did the instructor keep your interest at a high level?

   ❑ practically all the time ❑ part of the time ❑ seldom, if at all

   Comments _____

7. What percentage of the course was learning by doing on your part? _____%
   What was the nature of the "doing"?

   _____

8. The use of visual aids (chart, posters, slides, films, etc.) was:

   ❑ good ❑ fair ❑ non-existent

SAMPLE #7 — Continued

Type of visual aids used: _____

_____

9. Were practical examples and actual experiences cited to highlight theory?
   ❏ many ❏ some ❏ hardly any

10. Did the instructor get pertinent discussion going or did he or she do all the talking?
    ❏ considerable discussion ❏ fair amount ❏ little or none

11. Did the instructor use simple language or did he or she talk "over everyone's heads"?
    ❏ easily understood ❏ fair ❏ talked over our heads

12. How will this program help you improve your performance on your present job and/or help you prepare for increased responsibility?

_____

_____

13. Give a short summary statement of your general impression of the program, including both its strong points and weak points.

_____

_____

14. Based on what you learned during the training:

   a. What specific things are you going to do to improve results in your job or department?

   _____

   _____

   b. What specific recommendations do you have for improvements outside your job or department?

   _____

   _____

15. Should this company send additional personnel to this program? ❏ Yes ❏ No
    If yes, who do you think would benefit from it? (Give job titles, not names)

_____

_____

Additional comments: (attach extra page if necessary)

_____

_____

Reviewed by Manager: _____ Date: _____
Reviewed by Human Resources: _____ Date: _____

9
GENERAL RULES AND POLICIES

No society can function without rules. As we've already discussed, a company is, in effect, a minisociety. And just as with the larger society within which we all live, the small, corporate society must have rules and guidelines for employees to abide by. Without these rules, confusion, misunderstandings, and chaos can result.

a. RULES AND REGULATIONS

What are the rules that you feel are critical to the successful functioning of your company? What actions must you prohibit? What actions will be cause for disciplinary procedures? What rules must be put into place for efficient operations?

No two companies will come up with the same list of guidelines for its employees. The guidelines you develop will be based on your own unique corporate culture. The following list contains a number of areas of concern your handbook might include.

Breach of confidentiality or security:

- Discussing confidential matters with anyone outside the company or with unauthorized company associates. This includes discussing information contained in associate computer files
- Carrying concealed weapons on company property or concealing a weapon on company property
- Allowing unauthorized persons access to the building without permission of your manager
- Using, duplicating, or possessing keys to the building or offices within the building without authorization
- Removing company records
- Creating an oral or written statement defaming, ridiculing, degrading, or otherwise discrediting the company, its practices or its products
- Accessing computers or computer files of any associate without authorization

Theft or misuse of company time or resources:

- Stealing or attempting to steal property of the company, its customers, or another associate of the company
- Intentionally misusing or damaging company property
- Conducting personal business during working hours
- Making or receiving long-distance personal calls on company telephone lines
- Using the company's postage meter or postage stamps for personal reasons
- Using company stationery to write personal letters
- Misusing company vehicles, including personal use without permission of the President
- Making unauthorized purchases for the company

Improper work habits:

- Unauthorized working of overtime or failure to record overtime worked (non-exempt associates only)
- Failing to keep busy when there is work to be done
- Stretching breaks or otherwise wasting time
- Restricting output or engaging in any intentional slowdown or work stoppage
- Punching the time card or filling out the time sheet of another employee
- Improperly recording hours worked
- Stopping work before the shift ends

Discrimination or harassment:

- Deliberately or willfully violating the company's equal employment opportunity program
- Threatening, intimidating, coercing, harassing, or assaulting another associate at any time
- Sexual harassing of any kind.

Unsafe behavior:

- Bringing intoxicants or drugs, or consuming intoxicants or drugs (other than drugs prescribed by a physician) on the premises, or reporting to work under the influence of drugs or alcohol
- Failing to maintain a clean, sanitary, and safe workplace including littering or contributing to unsafe working conditions on company premises
- Refusing to wear personal protective equipment required for your safety by the company (Includes inconsistent use of such equipment.)

General unacceptable behavior:

- Failing to carry out any reasonable request of a superior
- Being frequently absent or tardy
- Disregarding personal appearance or hygiene
- Smoking in undesignated areas
- Consuming food outside of designated areas
- Soliciting associates and distributing literature on company premises or while any associate is working
- Soliciting contributions on company premises without authorization
- Accepting unauthorized gifts from businesses or individuals related to employment
- Providing false or misleading information on employment application
- Exhibiting any behavior that is unethical or dishonest in relation to your employment at the company
- Doing anything that causes the company's competitive position to diminish

Following are common ways of clarifying some of the above issues so that employees don't misunderstand you or make mistakes.

1. **Personnel records**

   Keep your personnel records up to date. Notify the Human Resources Manager of any change in your home address, telephone number, marital status, number of dependents, or other relevant personal data. If the information in your file is not correct, problems may arise concerning your taxes, employee benefits, and other important matters.

2. **Telephone procedures**

   Personal phone calls (incoming and outgoing) during business hours are to be kept to a minimum. Personal long-distance calls are to be billed to your home number. Calls made from the office before 8:00 a.m. and after 5:00 p.m. cost significantly less than calls made during other times of the day. When your business calls deal with other time zones, you are encouraged to consider making these calls before 8:00 a.m. or after 5:00 p.m.

3. Business gifts

The company prohibits associates from accepting gifts or gratuities from individuals or companies with whom we do business (or companies who would like to do business with us). Violation of this rule could result in termination. When in doubt whether to accept a gift in a business-related situation, check with your manager immediately. If a company or an individual gives you something in the capacity of your employment, it becomes the property of the company.

4. Personal property

The company assumes no responsibility or liability for associates' personal property that is lost or stolen on company premises or while you are on company business.

5. Company property

It is necessary to obtain approval from the president before removing any company property from the office for personal use. Unauthorized removal is a very serious matter and will be treated as such.

6. Contributions for gifts

Requests for contributions toward the purchase of gifts for fellow associates are restricted to a maximum of $5. In the event of birthdays, weddings, births, etc., we suggest that someone within the celebrating associate's department volunteer to collect money and purchase the gift. An announcement at the staff meeting should be made regarding this and the date by which the contribution should be made. No one is in any way required to contribute money for this purpose.

7. Other contributions

Requests to solicit for contributions to charitable organizations or causes must be approved by your division director. (This includes raffles, benefits, and school sales.) You may announce your approved contribution solicitation at a staff meeting, but you will not be permitted to disrupt the office by direct solicitation. Direct solicitation is prohibited during your or other associates' regular scheduled hours.

8. Personal mail

Personal mail, including magazines, should be sent to your home address and not to this business address. You may place your personal mail to be sent out in the mailbox by the reception desk. Make sure you have placed a stamp on it, since the company will not pay for mailing your personal correspondence.

9. Automobile liability coverage

Associates who operate their own or company vehicles on company business are covered by our liability insurance. This insurance is intended to protect the company from liability or damages resulting from accidents caused by associates driving on company business. This coverage does not absolve associates from their own negligence, nor does it provide any insurance protection to associates while operating their own vehicles while traveling between work and home.

We require that anyone driving or riding in a company vehicle or performing company business in a personal vehicle wear a seat belt at any time the vehicle is in motion (in accordance with the laws of _____).

10. Traffic tickets and parking violations

It is expected that anyone driving on company business will observe all traffic and parking laws in the area in which they are traveling. Any violations of these laws and any fines that may result are the personal responsibility of the driver. This includes use of a company vehicle, a personal vehicle, or a rental car.

11. Alcohol and driving

Open containers of alcoholic beverages are strictly prohibited in any vehicle that is being used for company business. This includes the driver and any passengers. Likewise, it is understood that you will not operate any vehicle on company business while under the influence of alcoholic beverages.

b. SMOKING/CHEWING TOBACCO

Why are employers beginning to exhibit concern about the smoking problem? There are a number of reasons, including the following:

(a) *Complaints from nonsmokers.* It has become accepted for nonsmokers to assert their rights everywhere, including in the workplace. Nonsmokers no longer want to tolerate secondhand smoke. They've begun to fight back. And, as the number of nonsmoking employees grow, they have become a force to be reckoned with.

(b) *Growing public awareness.* You can hardly pick up a newspaper or magazine or turn on the television set without hearing something about the hazards of smoking. In a society that's becoming more and more concerned about health, it's no longer "in" to smoke — it's "in" not to.

(c) *Legislation.* Some areas have specific laws governing smoking in the private workplace. These are laws that employers can't ignore.

(d) *Lawsuits.* Yes, smoking is another area that has come to the attention of the courts in our litigious society. Recently, an employee took her employer to court because she had developed obstructive lung disease due to, according to the suit, regular exposure to tobacco smoke during her ten years of employment. While the trial court was not convinced that she could sue her employer, the court of appeals later ruled that she could maintain her legal action.

(e) *Worker's compensation and unemployment claims.* If employers can't provide a risk-free work environment (and in more and more cases this means smoke-free), employees may be eligible for worker's compensation or disability benefits. Unemployment benefits have been awarded both to employees who feel that secondhand smoke in the workplace has injured their health and to those who have a "reasonable belief" that this smoke threatens their future health.

Smoking has become a major health issue — and not only for those who smoke. Hence the hue and cry over the ill effects of smoking in the workplace. Employees who are sensitive to tobacco smoke may suffer eye, nose, and throat irritation, headaches, and nausea. Secondhand smoke can also contribute to emphysema and lung disease. These troubling physical effects for nonsmokers constitutes a "handicap" and, just as with any other type of handicap, employers are obligated to "reasonably accommodate" these employees. How? Any number of ways — relocating the employee's workstation, restructuring the job, providing the employee with an air filter or fan, or banning smoking in the workplace altogether.

In your handbook, you should include a statement about the company's smoking/nonsmoking policy. Indicate whether tobacco use is permitted, and if so, where and when.

> The company discourages its associates from smoking and chewing tobacco because these are regarded as poor health habits. Smoking and chewing are permitted, however, during morning and afternoon breaks and during lunch periods but are limited to the patio area adjacent to the break room.

c. DRUG/ALCOHOL ABUSE

Another issue that has received increasing attention in recent years is that of the effects of drug and alcohol abuse on employee performance — and safety. Drug use has been shown to increase industrial accidents including property damage and personal injury. In addition, drug use can lower productivity and increase absenteeism and tardiness.

One of the ways some companies have chosen to fight drug abuse is through drug testing. This, in itself, has become a major issue from boardrooms to loading docks across the continent.

Naturally, employers want to protect themselves, their clientele, and other employees from the adverse affects of an employee who abuses illicit drugs. Just as naturally, employees are concerned about their right to privacy, about misread or incorrect test results, and about the effects of all of this on their current and future earning capacity.

The decision to implement a drug-use testing program should be made only after careful consideration. Safety issues are paramount and must drive such a decision. Employers should review the legal issues involved in making such a move in addition to the employee relations issues that will, no doubt, arise and may have an adverse impact on employee morale and productivity.

Be aware of what drug-use testing can and cannot do. Certain tests may not be admissible in court in the event of a wrongful discharge suit.

If you're considering the establishment of a drug-free work force program, make sure that you —

(a) are aware of federal, state/provincial, and local requirements applying to drug testing;

(b) consider the possible application of general handicap discrimination laws that may apply to rehabilitated drug users;

(c) consider the issues of accuracy, confidentiality, and employee privacy, and how they may affect claims of abusive discharge; and

(d) consider the subjective impact of such a decision on your work force.

> All new job applicants who have received a conditional offer of employment must show themselves to be free from the presence of illegal drugs through a drug screening test. The job offer is withdrawn if the medical review officer upholds findings of a confirmed positive test.
>
> An employee may be required to report to a designated physician or

health care provider for a fitness-for-duty examination if the person appears unfit for duty, or when a supervisor determines there is reasonable cause that the employee has violated the company drug and alcohol policy. The fitness-for-duty examination may include drug and alcohol screening. Fitness-for-duty exams that are positive but are not policy violations will not subject the employee to discipline; however, if appropriate, modifications and/or restrictions of work assignments will be imposed.

Employees completing a required chemical dependency rehabilitation program will be subject to post-treatment follow-up monitoring for up to two years, or as required by federal regulations.

Employees and job applicants have the right to submit additional information to explain a confirmed drug screen result to the medical review officer within three working days of test result notification. Employees and job applicants also may request in writing a copy of drug screen results and/or a retest of the original sample at an approved laboratory of their choice within five working days of test result notification. The results of the retest will be binding.

The company strongly supports employee actions to responsibly resolve substance abuse problems. Accordingly, we encourage employees to work through our employee-assistance program toward a resolution of the problem and will consider employee requests for a 90-day unpaid leave of absence to treat a health problem.

If your company does not test for drug use, you might still consider alternatives for dealing with the problem of drug and alcohol use and abuse. These alternatives might include education and training programs designed to combat abuse, increased security and surveillance, rehabilitation, and employee assistance. The following wording is appropriate for a company that does not have a drug-testing policy.

Because alcoholism and drug dependency are recognized health problems, early recognition and treatment are necessary to the welfare of the employee and the company. We offer assistance when drinking or drug abuse keeps employees from performing their duties satisfactorily or makes them display unbecoming conduct.

In the event of such problems, the employee, supervisor, or family members can get help through the employee-assistance program with complete confidentiality. There will be no adverse effect on the career of an employee who seeks treatment.

Employees shall not use alcohol or other mood-altering chemicals during normal working hours. For the purpose of this policy, "normal working hours" include breaks and meal periods. This policy excludes a doctor's prescription used as prescribed. Employees shall not report for work unable to perform their duties as a result of using alcohol and/or mood-altering chemicals. These substances are not permitted in or on company property.

Whether an employee drinks alcoholic beverages at times other than working hours is generally the individual's personal business, but there may be times when it is the company's business as well. If drinking or use of other moodaltering chemicals leads to unsatisfactory performance, excessive absenteeism, a poor safety record or misconduct, then the company is directly concerned and will take appropriate disciplinary action.

d. OUTSIDE EMPLOYMENT (MOONLIGHTING)

As an employer you are not in a position to control what your employees do outside of the office. However, you do have a right to be concerned about their readiness for work when they are under your employ. Frequently the issue of moonlighting comes up. How can you address this issue without seeming as though you're attempting to control your employees outside of their work hours? Include a statement in your personnel handbook to the effect that:

> If you feel that your circumstances are such that you need (or want) to accept outside employment, you are asked to discuss the matter with your manager before doing so. The company has no objection to your accepting a second job unless it has a negative effect on your ability to satisfy the job-related requirements of your position, is in direct competition with our business, or involves the use of confidential information learned directly or indirectly through your employment with the company. You are requested to discuss the second job with your manager to help you to determine whether there is any possibility of a conflict of interest or a breach of confidentiality.

e. CONFIDENTIAL NATURE OF BUSINESS

We work in a competitive environment and it is not at all unlikely that there are aspects of your business and its operations that you consider to be confidential. To avoid any misunderstandings on this point you may want to include a statement on confidentiality in your handbook.

Many of the business topics discussed, memos distributed or posted, business contacts, and other information made available to associates in the normal course of their jobs are confidential. These include information about product development, production schedules of any sort, information about upcoming projects, corporate goals and whether or not they are attained, and debts, revenue, or income from any project or product or of the company as a whole.

In connection with the above, it is the responsibility of every associate to be sure that competitors do not receive information in any form that will be to the company's competitive disadvantage. Therefore, it is inappropriate for employees to discuss these company activities outside of the business setting, and never with anyone associated or connected with a competitor without the permission of a director.

To further safeguard confidential information, documents, reports, or any writing containing information on the above should not be taken from the building without permission from a manager. In addition, any document, report or schedule stamped "trade secret" should be treated with the highest degree of care and should not be copied without permission or shown to anyone who is not an associate.

The company reserves any and all legal rights it has against associates for violating trade secrets under law. No person having any interest, association, or relationship with any organization that in any way competes with the company in its production of products or delivery of services will be allowed access to the building except for the reception area, without permission from one of the directors or the owner.

f. SEXUAL HARASSMENT

Sexual harassment is a serious situation and should not be taken lightly. To discourage harassing behavior and encourage those who are victimized to report the problem, you should include a firm, clear statement on your sexual harassment policies.

1. It is illegal and against the company's policy for any worker, male or female, to harass another worker by making unwelcome sexual advances or engaging in other unwelcome verbal or physical conduct of a sexual nature, using an associate's submission to or rejection of such conduct as the basis for or as a factor in any employment decision affecting the individual, or otherwise creating an intimidating, hostile, or offensive working environment by such conduct.

2. The creation of an intimidating, hostile, or offensive working environment may include actions such as persistent comments on an associate's sexual preferences or the display of obscene or sexually oriented photographs or drawings.

3. We recognize that some conduct or actions arise out of a personal or social relationship and may not be intended to have a discriminatory employment effect. Depending on the circumstances, this conduct may or may not be viewed as harassment. The management will determine whether such conduct constitutes sexual harassment, based on a review of the facts and circumstances of each situation.

4. The company will not condone any sexual harassment of its associates. All associates, including managers and directors, will be subject to discipline up to and including discharge for any substantiated act of sexual harassment they commit.

5. Associates who feel victimized by sexual harassment should report the harassment to their manager immediately. If the associate's manager is the source of the alleged harassment, the associate should report the problem to his or her director, the Human Resources Manager, or one of the owners immediately.

6. Managers and directors who receive a sexual harassment complaint should consult with the Human Resources Manager, who will carefully investigate the matter. Special privacy safeguards will be applied in handling this type of complaint. The Human Resources Manager will question all associates who may have knowledge of either the incident in question or similar problems. The complaint, the investigative steps, and all findings will be documented as thoroughly as possible.

7. Associates who are dissatisfied with the resolution of a sexual harassment complaint may file a complaint through the company's problem resolution procedure.

No associate will be subject to any form of retaliation or discipline for pursuing a sexual harassment complaint.

g. INFECTIOUS DISEASES

Employees who have an infectious disease can pose a threat to everyone in your company and to anyone who comes into contact with the company. On the other hand, some "infectious" diseases are not dangerous to others under normal working conditions. A typical policy on employees with infectious diseases might include the following wording:

> This policy has been established in an effort to protect the company's employees and customers from infectious diseases. The company recognizes that many employees with health-threatening infections desire to lead normal lives, which includes working as long as they are able.
>
> Employees are encouraged to continue working as long as they are able to perform and their illness presents no threat to themselves, other employees, or customers. Employees who know they have an infectious disease should not engage in any activity that creates a risk of transmission of the disease to others.
>
> The manager, director, or Human Resources Manager should be notified that an employee has an infectious disease. The president, director, and Human Resources Manager will determine whether an associate can adequately and safely perform duties. They may confer with the employee's personal physician in making the decision. The result may be a change in work assignment, a disability layoff, or termination. (Termination may be justified if the associate's condition poses a medical risk of contagion to others.)
>
> Employees with AIDS or other life-threatening infections are entitled to the same employment benefits as other workers in the organization who have medical problems. The company will do what it can to try to ensure that employees are provided with competent medical care and counseling where needed. All medical records of employees are strictly confidential.
>
> The company reserves the right to require an employee to undergo a medical examination by a doctor chosen by the company whenever there is a question of an employee's fitness to work or where there is reason to fear that an employee's condition might pose safety or health hazards for other associates.
>
> The company will make reasonable job accommodations where necessary to assist associates with life-threatening infections.

h. PROBLEM RESOLUTION

Any time people come together in a group situation, conflicts and complaints are apt to arise on occasion. For this reason, you may want to include a section in your handbook dealing with problem resolution. Where does an employee go when he or she has a complaint or problem? What recourse is available to employees who feel they have suffered some injustice?

> If there is something bothering you related to your employment, or to company policies or practices, please feel free to bring it out in the open. Every effort will be made to address your concern. If we don't know about it, we can't do anything to correct it. Following are the steps you should take to have your problem or concern addressed:
>
> 1. *Talk to your immediate supervisor.** Talk over your problem honestly and sincerely. There is a good possibility that your problem can be resolved at this stage. You may also wish to discuss the situation with your manager at this point.
>
> 2. *Inform the Human Resources Manager.* If your problem remains unre-

solved, talk to the Human Resources Manager. It will be reviewed again and discussed with you. If solutions still are not found, go to step 3.

3. *Speak to the president.* At this point, you will meet with the Human Resources Manager and the president for a complete and fair hearing. A final decision will be reached, the reasoning for this decision will be documented in writing, and a copy will be given to you.

*If you are not comfortable talking with your immediate supervisor, feel free to speak with your supervisor's manager, the Human Resources Manager, or the president.

i. DISCIPLINARY PROCEDURES

Many companies outline in their handbooks the steps they will take when dealing with rule infractions or other disciplinary issues. This is an area where caution should be exercised. By no means do you want to give the impression that you will follow a strict path from verbal warning through written warning to dismissal in every case. You will want to reserve the right to begin disciplinary action at any step you deem applicable. The following statement included in your handbook can help you avoid potential problems:

> Whether or not disciplinary procedures against associates are taken by the management of the company in no way will the right of the company to discharge an employee at any time for any or no reason be negated. It is impossible to categorically state when or if disciplinary measures or termination of the employment relationship will be appropriate action. However, if disciplinary action is taken, it is the company's intent that the discipline will serve to correct employee behavior rather than to serve solely as a penalty for a past offense.
>
> At the company's sole discretion, various types of employee discipline may be imposed that include, but are not limited to, the following: informal warning, counseling, verbal reprimand, written warning, or suspension. None of these disciplinary measures is required to be used before termination from employment occurs nor are the listed disciplinary actions required to be used in any specific order.

What should an employee do if he or she feels action has been taken that is unfair? What if there are extenuating circumstances? Having an appeals procedure will demonstrate to your employees that you wish to be fair-minded and that your goal is to come to an equitable resolution of any problem and not necessarily to assess blame and apply sanctions.

> If you honestly feel that the circumstances surrounding a disciplinary action are unfair, you may start the appeal process. We hope that this procedure will be used only as a last resort because of the seriousness of the issues involved. Every effort should be made to work out differences with your manager and/or director first.
>
> 1. Appeals must be submitted to the Human Resources Manager in writing not more than seven days following the disciplinary action. Your appeal will be heard and decided by the Human Resources Manager and the president.
>
> 2. Within seven days of your starting the appeal process, you will meet with the Human Resources Manager and president and conduct a thorough and objective

review of the problem. The decision reached by them is final and binding.

j. COVER YOUR BASES

The area of rule coverage in employee handbooks can be a tricky one. While you want to let employees know what actions will not be tolerated, you can't possibly hope to cover all of the various infractions that might be cause for discipline or dismissal. This is an area where you can find yourself in legal trouble unless you clearly state the purpose of your regulations in a manner similar to the following:

> While it is impossible to list all the rules employees are expected to follow, some of the more serious infractions that will subject you to discipline (up to and including termination) are outlined here. This list is not meant to be all-inclusive. Management reserves the right to terminate employees for any reason, at any time. All employees are expected to abide by these rules.

10
LEGAL CONSIDERATIONS

The best advice I can give about developing a personnel handbook is: DON'T. The logic is that for everything you spell out there are five things you'll miss which can be construed [by contingency fee lawyers] in a manner unhealthy for your business. Little traps like listing a few grounds for dismissal, then having all the grounds not listed being considered invalid. Like having an AIDS policy, but not a hepatitis policy, etc. In short, leave handbooks to the pros or leave them alone.

This statement was made by a business owner and expresses a common feeling. Many small — and large — business owners feel much the same way. And there is basis for their trepidation. Employee handbooks can open your company to potential legal problems. But so can the lack of an employee handbook.

a. WATCH YOUR LANGUAGE

The key to avoiding these problems is to understand where the potential for trouble lies. The problem with many personnel handbooks is that by including certain statements they challenge the "employment-at-will" concept and make it difficult, to legally discipline or terminate employees.

The employment-at-will doctrine is a legal concept that has been followed on a widespread basis. Employment-at-will means that either a company or an employer can terminate an employment relationship at any time for any reason that is not illegal. The most obvious exceptions are the following:

(a) An employer cannot terminate an employee if that termination would violate anti-discrimination laws.

(b) An employer cannot terminate an employee for any situation that would contravene public policy (for instance an employee could not be fired for refusing a superior's order to break the law).

Employment-at-will has traditionally meant that employers have the right to terminate employees whose performance is not up to standard. Employment relationships were interpreted to be "non-permanent."

A poorly drafted handbook can change this relationship. For instance, if your handbook lists specific work rules, a court could determine that an employee could not be disciplined for something that is not included. Or, if your handbook contains a progressive disciplinary procedure, your company could be in legal jeopardy if you fail to adhere strictly to these procedures.

The proper language can help you avoid these problems and throughout this book we provide you with examples of non-compromising wording for you to use in your personnel manual, for example:

> This list is intended as an example only and is not intended to indicate all of those acts that could lead to employee discipline.

or

This progressive disciplinary policy is intended as a guideline only. An action could start at any point in the process, including immediate termination.

To avoid legal problems with your handbook, consider the following tips.

1. Promises, promises...

Don't make promises in the handbook that you don't intend to keep. For instance, don't state in your handbook that all employees will be "reviewed twice a year: in March and September," unless you intend to adhere religiously to this statement.

Watch out for implied promises both in your handbook and in statements made by you or your employees. The type of statements to be wary of? Any dealing with implications about guaranteed job security or advancement opportunities could cause problems. So could statements about *probationary* vs. *permanent* employment status. Such statements might be interpreted to mean that once an employee has worked for a specified period of time he or she is guaranteed a job for life.

Stay away from wishy-washy language like, "We will be fair to our employees." The term "fair" is open to interpretation and can get you into trouble.

2. Revise regularly

Revise your employee handbook regularly. Be aware of the rules and regulations governing your jurisdiction. Laws vary by state or province — sometimes even by county. Laws can change so dramatically within a short period of time that you may be liable to a lawsuit if the appropriate sections in your handbook are not modified. Know the rules that affect you and stay current on the changes in those rules.

Keep your job descriptions up to date and tied to the actual requirements of the job. Outdated job descriptions can lead to problems if discharged employees claim they were terminated for failure to do work for which they were not originally hired.

3. Don't limit yourself

When discussing reasons for termination decisions in your handbook watch for references to dismissal only for "just cause" or vague terms like "fair" that could cause you problems later. The following qualifying statement would be appropriate to include in your handbook:

> We recognize our employees' rights to resign at any time for any reason; similarly we may terminate any employee at any time, with or without cause. No one other than the company owner has the authority to modify this relationship or to make any agreements to the contrary. Any such modification or agreement must be in writing.

Do include a list of potential cause for discharge though. Such a list can help alleviate employee fears about arbitrary dismissal. But make sure that you also include a statement to the effect that this list is intended to be a "guideline only" and that management retains the right to discharge an employee for any reason. This language might read as follows:

> While it is impossible to list all the rules associates are expected to follow, some of the more serious infractions that will subject you to discipline (up to and including termination) are outlined herein. This list is not meant to be all-inclusive. Management reserves the right to terminate associates for any reason, at any time.

This language may seem harsh and may certainly be cause for concern among your employees. It is necessary to include, though, to protect yourself and your company — to help allay some fears, explain to your employees why you must include such language.

Be cautious when outlining layoff procedures. Today's business climate has made "downsizing" and reductions in work forces a fact of life and one that your company may, unfortunately, have to deal with. Statements included in your handbook related to this issue should avoid indications that layoff decisions will be based on length of service. You will want to retain the right to terminate employees based on performance — not seniority.

4. Subject to change...

You will also want to indicate in your handbook that the information contained can be changed or modified at any time.

> Management reserves the right to change the provisions of this handbook at any time, with or without notice. In almost all cases, changes to the handbook will be announced in a timely fashion.

b. THE HANDBOOK AS A CONTRACTUAL DOCUMENT

> The contents of this handbook are presented as a matter of information of employment only. This handbook does not constitute an express or implied contract for employment. It provides guidelines only and may be changed or disregarded when, in the opinion of management, circumstances so require.

An employee handbook is viewed as a contractual document in most locales. Because of this, it is especially critical that you carefully consider each statement you include in the handbook so you don't obligate yourself to meet conditions that you are not prepared to meet.

To help avoid some of the inherent contractual problems with employee handbooks, many companies include disclaimer statements at critical points in the handbook itself. Some of these points might include the following:

(a) The introduction

(b) The discussion of orientation or training periods

(c) The section on complaint or dispute resolution

(d) In the listing of standards of conduct and work rules

(e) As part of the statement acknowledging receipt of the handbook by the employee

Such disclaimers should appear prominently when they are included and should not be buried in the text or printed in such small type that attention is diverted from them.

Following is an example of a statement of purpose that might be included in the introduction to a personnel handbook. Notice that language is included in this statement relating to the rights of employees conferred by the handbook and touching on certain legal issues. This same type of language could be included in other parts of your handbook and might serve to protect you from various legal problems that sometimes develop based on implications of a "right to employment" or contractual agreement:

> This handbook has been produced by the company for the guidance and orientation of our employees. None of the benefits or polices in this handbook is intended by reason of publication to confer any rights or privileges, or to entitle you to be or to remain to be employed by the company. The contents of this handbook are presented as a matter of information of employment only.
>
> This handbook does not constitute an express or implied contract for employment. It provides guidelines only and may be changed or disregarded when, in the opinion of management, circumstances so require. Management reserves the right to change the provisions of this

handbook at any time, with or without notice. In almost all cases, changes to the handbook will be announced in a timely fashion. We will use one, some, or all of the following to announce changes when needed: staff meeting, department or division meetings, memos, and the bulletin board. However, we retain the right to implement some changes immediately without advance notice.

Each manager is responsible for maintaining a completely updated copy of this handbook available to all employees at all times. Copies of all changes will also be distributed to all associates, and it will be up to you to make sure your handbook is current. In the event of a dispute, the most recently updated and announced version will be used. All changes will be issued through the Human Resources Department; however, no one other than the president has the authority to effect changes pertaining to the plans, policies, or procedures described herein. Any changes must be in writing.

We recognize our employees' rights to resign at any time for any reason; similarly we may terminate any employee at any time, with or without cause. No one other than the president has the authority to modify this relationship or to make any agreements to the contrary. Any such modification or agreement must be in writing.

A statement to the effect that "this handbook does not constitute an express or implied contract for employment" is important to include because it can dissuade employees from suing and will be sufficient evidence of intent in most locales. However, in a lawsuit, the matter of whether or not the handbook was a contract can be open to interpretation by the court, even if such language is included.

In addition to the language concerning the lack of any implied employment contract, this statement also illustrates two other points about the handbook: communicating changes and modifications and the responsibility of the manager to maintain an updated version of the handbook.

In your handbook, you will also want to make explicit the rights and responsibilities your company has in relation to dealing with employees. The following statement provides an example of the type of language you might use:

> Certain rights and responsibilities are imposed on the company by state/provincial and federal legislation and court decisions. Many of these have implications for polices and procedures governing employment. For this reason, please be advised that we hereby reserve any and all management rights regarding employees' employment status. These rights and responsibilities include, but are not limited to, the following:
>
> To manage and direct company employees, including hiring, promotion, scheduling, transfers, assignment or retention of employees in positions within the company and to establish work rules; to lay off employees; to discharge or take other appropriate disciplinary action when necessary; to schedule overtime work as required consistent with the requirements of the company; to develop job descriptions, bearing in mind that such descriptions are usually guidelines and not rigid limitations and that associates shall perform any reasonable assigned duties; to introduce new or improved methods or facilities or to

change existing methods or facilities; to fulfill its obligations in contracting out for matters relating to the operation of the company; to discontinue certain operations; and, to direct all questions of the company.

c. THE LEGAL REVIEW

Employee handbooks are complex documents and subject to interpretation by employees and the courts. To avoid legal liability, always have these documents reviewed by a lawyer. If you have legal counsel on staff, that may suffice. However, you will be best served by a lawyer who specializes in employment law. You can locate such a lawyer through your local bar association, legal referral service, or legal directory at your library.

Fees for reviewing your manual will vary depending on your locale; however, expect to pay between $50 and $100 per hour. View this fee as insurance against potential lawsuits that could carry with them exorbitant legal fees as well as costly judgments if your handbook is not legally sound.

PART III
PRESENTING YOUR INFORMATION

11
DESIGN AND LAYOUT

If your handbook isn't "usable" it won't be used. It's as simple as that. To be usable, your handbook needs to be attractively produced and easy to read. It needs to be well organized so that employees can quickly turn to the sections that interest them or about which they have questions.

In this chapter, we take a look at ways you can make your handbook attractive and easy to use through design and layout considerations and some simple organizational techniques.

Once you've gathered all of the information you need, determined which policies, procedures, and guidelines to include, and reached a consensus on how to word those sections, the next step is actually preparing the handbook.

a. FORMAT

First you'll want to determine a format that is most appropriate for you and your company. There are basically three formats you might decide to use, although there are certainly a number of variations for each. These formats are perfect-bound (like a paperback book), three-ring binder, and automated (on computer). Automated handbooks and their special requirements are discussed in section **g.** below.

1. Perfect-bound

If your handbook is unlikely to change on a regular basis, you may find that perfect binding is a less expensive — and more efficient format for you. Why? With perfect binding you avoid the additional cost of a binder and the labor cost of punching and assembling your handbooks. However, if your handbook is likely to change frequently, or if the number of copies you will need is small, perfect binding may not be a cost-effective or practical option for you.

If you do decide to use a perfect-bound format, one option available to you to accommodate changes is to have a flap included on the front or back cover of the book so that changes can be printed and easily slipped in. They will obviously not be able to be placed into the correct spot in the book, but the flap will allow you the option of preparing material that can stay with the book and be incorporated into a future printing.

2. Three-ring binder

A three-ring binder offers the flexibility to change pages easily — without having to reprint the entire book. And, if you have a relatively small number of handbooks to produce, a three-ring format would allow you to actually produce the copies in-house with your office copier and a three-hole punch. While you would have to forego some of the aesthetic values you could obtain through a commercial printer, this option may be a practical one when you first introduce your handbook. At this early stage, it's likely that you would find the need to make a number of modifications as the handbook is put into use.

In larger quantities, a three-ring binder may not be the most cost-effective option. Another potential problem of the three-ring binder format is that when you simply hand out loose pages to employees you cannot be assured that their books are, at any given time, completely up to date. If they fail to add or change pages as you instruct, you run the risk of having a number of outdated handbooks with incorrect information in active circulation within your company.

One way to overcome this potential problem is to hold a meeting with all employees (or require each department to hold such a meeting) where they are required to bring their existing handbooks. At the meeting the new pages can be passed out, old pages can be collected, and you can be satisfied that all handbooks are up to date.

3. Focus on your company's needs

Whether you choose perfect-bound or binder format, you still have to decide just how elaborate you want your manual to be. The simplest handbook would be one prepared on a typewriter or word processor and this is certainly an option. It serves the purpose of getting the information out to employees and it has the benefit of being able to be prepared and easily updated in-house by existing staff.

On the other end of the spectrum is the professionally designed handbook which might make use of two or more colors, glossy paper, striking graphics, even photography.

The route you take will depend on your budget and the needs and culture of your organization. A small, new company may be justifiably leery of the expense of producing a very expensive employee handbook. A larger company, on the other hand, may feel only the best is good enough.

In the following discussion we take the middle ground and assume that you either have access to and experience with a desktop publishing system or that you can work with a local freelancer to provide some expertise in this area.

b. SIZE

What size will your handbook be? While you can choose any size that you feel is appropriate, the most common is 8½ x 11 for a couple of reasons:

(a) It's the most obvious size for a three-ring binder format which is what most companies decide to use. An 8½ x 11 size permits easy substitution of old pages with new.

(b) 8½ x 11 is a common printing size and does not require the ordering of special paper or additional costs incurred through trimming paper to a different size. It is also the most common size for photocopy paper, so if you choose that route for reproducing your handbook, you won't have any difficulty.

(c) Most of the forms you use in your business and that you may want to illustrate or include in your handbook will be 8½ x 11. By printing the handbook itself in this size you avoid the necessity to shrink forms to a small (and potentially illegible) size.

(d) If you are preparing the pages for your handbook on a word processor or typewriter, the default page setting will be 8½ x 11.

We will assume, then, that you will be working with an 8½ x 11 format as you prepare your handbook.

c. PAGE NUMBERING

Carefully consider how you will number the pages in your handbook. For instance, if you use a standard sequential numbering system, from 1 to 999, for example, and later want to add pages in the middle of your manual, you will either have to renumber and reissue all subsequent pages or resort to using 3a, 3b, 3c, etc.

A better choice is to number the pages within each section or chapter. For instance, pages in chapter one might go 1-1, 1-2, 1-3, pages in chapter two, 2-1, 2-2. If pages are added or deleted, you will only have to renumber and reissue one chapter instead of the whole manual.

In addition to a page number, each page should also include a date so users can quickly determine when the information was last updated.

d. FINDING AND WORKING WITH OUTSIDE DESIGN HELP

1. Choosing a designer

Whether your company is headquartered in a large or a small community, you're sure to be able to find qualified design assistance near you. One way of finding this help is to put an ad in the local paper as you would for any other position you needed to fill. Other ways might include:

- contacting the local college or technical schools — they can often refer you to students who have the skills you need;
- contacting local businesses — they may be able to provide you with leads; or
- asking your employees if they know people who have the skills you need.

Once you have located some potential sources of assistance, you will want to interview these candidates just as you would for any other job. The only difference is that, unlike in many other jobs, you will be able to see with your own eyes whether the candidates have the skills and abilities to do the job you need to have done.

Request that each candidate bring with them to the interview examples of work they have done in the past, particularly work on other employee handbooks or similar materials — annual reports, newsletters, etc.

Review these materials carefully during your meeting and ask questions to determine how involved the designer was in the project. Did the designer come up with the format or was it developed by someone else? How much of the design is original and how much was created through the use of clip art? What did the designer like about each project? Dislike? What would the designer do differently today?

You'll want to pay close attention to the style of the designer. If the samples you see are very flamboyant and your company is more sedate and reserved, you may want to look elsewhere. Conversely, if the designer's style is very structured and traditional and your company culture is unrestrained or cutting edge, you may want to seek someone who mirrors more closely the style of your organization.

2. Making the most of freelance talent

When working with a freelancer, it's important that you know what you want and provide specific direction to the person you're working with. This will help avoid potential problems, disagreements, and disasters. The more precisely you can indicate what you're looking for, the more likely you are to get what you want.

You need to very clearly indicate what you expect from the person who will be performing this job and determine what the person expects of you (What background material will you provide? What equipment will you make available for the freelancer's use? Will the freelancer be expected to be available for meetings with you or other representatives of your company? If so, how often and where?)

Know what you want when you make your initial assignment. If you continually change your mind, you will frustrate the person you're working with and run up higher tabs for the project.

And — the area where most problems arise — what are the payment arrangements? Will you be paying on an hourly or a project basis? If hourly, how will the person report those hours? If on a project basis, what reporting do you want along the way? What critical checkpoints will you want to monitor? What will be done in the event that the work is not what you expected? Not up to your standards? How can the agreement be terminated?

Put your requirements, payment agreements, and any other important elements of this relationship in writing so that both you and the freelancer have guidelines to follow and are clear about what is expected.

It's also important that someone in your company be designated as the person who will serve as the channel through which communications can move from the designer to others in your company and vice versa. This individual will need to keep up to date on progress, when the designer may be available for — or needed at — meetings, etc.

Guard against the propensity to fall victim to the "out-of-sight, out-of-mind" mentality. Keep close tabs on the progress of the project. If you're serving as the facilitator, make sure you make yourself available and that you are responsive to questions that arise.

While you will want to make sure that you give clear direction on the project and your goals, remain open to new ideas. Remember that you are paying for the designer's expertise and he or she may have a number of ideas to offer you. Don't stifle these ideas by being too directive or by meddling unnecessarily in the project.

e. DESIGN CONSIDERATIONS

The field of graphic design is a complex one and you will, no doubt, get the best results in your employee handbook by using a professional to aid you. However, with the advent of desktop publishing systems, more and more companies are choosing to assume some basic design responsibility on their own. If this is the case, or if you just want some basic background that will help in evaluating the work of the designers you will be contracting with, the following information should help you on your way.

First of all, remember that while attractive layout adds to the impact of your handbook, it cannot replace substance. Make sure you strive for a balance between the content and the "look" of your publication. Don't spend all your time and resources on the design and printing of the manual while neglecting to do a good job on the research and writing.

When choosing paper and ink, make sure the paper stock is sufficiently opaque. Since you'll most likely be printing on both sides of the page, you'll want to ensure that the ink doesn't show through from the other side.

To achieve a multi-color look without the expense of full-color printing, consider using a colored paper and/or ink. Just make sure there is enough contrast between the paper you choose and the color of ink(s) you use. White paper with black ink offers the most contrast, of course. If you use colored paper, choose a soft muted color that won't make the ink "muddy" and difficult to read.

For the inside of your handbook you'll want to use a dull, not glossy, paper stock.

Choose a type face that is easy to read. Scripts, cursives, etc. are difficult to read, as are sans serif faces (type without the "tails"). A serif face is best — New Century Schoolbook is a common choice and is available on most systems.

Use italics, bold facing, and other type "enhancers" sparingly. Desktop publishing has made it easy to embellish text but if you do it too much, the effect of emphasis will be lost.

Use subheads in pages where you have a great deal of text with no illustration.

Subheads help break up the copy and make it easier to read. Solid blocks of type can be offputting.

Use occasional *call outs* — a quote or phrase pulled out from the text and displayed in the margin or a box. These can be used effectively to emphasize major points.

Try to allow for a lot of *white space* — areas on the page where there is no type. Wide margins and plenty of space between lines and words can help you achieve an open, readable page.

f. FINDING AND WORKING WITH A PRINTER

If you are preparing your handbook yourself or if you have not asked the designer to work directly with a printer, you will need to make these arrangements on your own. The process is much the same as the one you used in selecting a designer. Ask around. What printers have other businesses used and how did they feel about the work? What samples of material printed can the various printers provide you with? How close do these samples mirror your needs?

You'll find that printers, in general, are eager to help you out. They understand that most of their customers are not familiar with printing jargon and will guide you through the process of making decisions about things such as type of paper to use, number of ink colors, use of half-tones (photographs), *bleeds* (ink that runs off the edge of the page), etc.

When deciding on a printer, you'll want to work with three or four to get an idea of the different types of services provided as well as the variations in price. Your goal is to get the best value and best product for your money. In the printing industry, this process of checking out printing services is done through competitive bidding. You provide each printer with an indication of the type of work you want done, the quantity and the delivery date, and they provide you with an estimated cost of production.

Sample #8 shows a bidding estimate form that you could modify to meet your needs. It contains the type of standard information that every printer will want to know about your job.

g. THE COMPUTERIZED HANDBOOK

An option that may be available to you if your employees all have ready access to a computer and if all computers are linked together through some kind of networking software, is to put your handbook "on line." This allows you to make changes on an up-to-the-minute basis, assures that all employees have access to the same information (and the correct information) at all times and saves you the cost of printing and reprinting a handbook.

The mere creation of a personnel manual data file doesn't automatically launch you into the world of effective computerization, however. Before you can do that, you need to develop an organized system for managing all of that data. This means coming up with ways to organize it, update and maintain it, and retrieve and manipulate it.

To avoid the pitfalls, keep the following tips in mind.

1. Gather information up front

The importance of good communication cannot be overemphasized. Make sure that you know what your needs are now and have a good idea of what your needs will be in the future. Make sure that everyone who will be using the system has had the opportunity for input. Develop a system that can coordinate all the varied needs of your company into an efficient database.

2. Garbage in — garbage out!

Any computer system is only as good as the data entered into it, so the second most important pitfall to avoid is sloppy maintenance of information. If you put garbage into your system, you will get only garbage out of it. The information in your computerized personnel handbook will lose its value quickly if it's incorrectly entered or sloppily maintained. It's a good idea to establish detailed procedures that include standards to be followed for such basics as adding new sections, deleting old sections, changing the organizational chart, etc.

Limit the number of people who have the ability to enter or change information and closely monitor and control this entry. Without these controls, your system can become inaccurate and worthless.

3. Provide adequate documentation

Good documentation is crucial. The people involved in the implementation of your system will, of course, be familiar with it and the requirements for making updates and changes. New employees, however, will need to be trained to operate the system, and to do this, you will need proper documentation.

Without sufficient documentation, you defeat the purpose of your computerized handbook and create confusion and potential liability when incorrect data is entered or changes are not implemented consistently.

SAMPLE #8
REQUEST FOR QUOTATION

Request for Quotation

Job name _____ Date _____

Contact person _____

Date quote needed _____

Business name _____

Date job to printer _____

Address _____

Date job needed _____

Phone _____

Please give ❑ firm quote ❑ rough estimate ❑ verbally ❑ in writing

This is a ❑ new job ❑ exact reprint ❑ reprint with changes

Quantity: (1)_____ (2)_____ (3)_____ ❑ additional_____

Quality: ❑ basic ❑ good ❑ premium ❑ showcase

Comments: _____

Format: product description _____

flat trim size _____x_____ folded/bound size _____x_____

# of pages _____ ❑ self cover ❑ plus cover

Design features: ❑ bleeds ❑ screen tints #_____ ❑ reverses

#_____

❑ comp enclosed

Art: ❑ camera-ready

❑ printer to typeset and paste up (manuscript and rough layout attached)

❑ plate-ready negatives with proofs to printer's specifications

Trade shop name and contact person _____

_____

Mechanicals: color breaks ❑ on acetate overlays ❑ shown on tissues

pieces separate line art _____

Half-tones: ❑ half-tones #_____ ❑ duotones #_____

Separations: ❑ from transparencies #_____

❑ from reflective copy #_____ ❑ provided #_____

Finished sizes of separations _____

SAMPLE #8 — Continued

Proofs: ❑ galley ❑ page ❑ blueline ❑ loose color ❑ composite color
❑ progressive

Paper: weight name color finish grade

cover _____

inside _____

❑ send samples of paper ❑ make dummy buy paper from _____

Printing ink color(s)/varnish ink color(s)/varnish

cover side 1_____side 2_____

inside side 1_____side 2_____

_____ side 1_____side 2_____

_____ side 1_____side 2_____

Ink ❑ special color match ❑ special ink_____ ❑ need draw down

coverage is ❑ light ❑ moderate ❑ heavy ❑ see comp attached ❑ need press check

Other printing (die cut, emboss, foil stamp, engrave, thermograph, number, etc.)

_____

_____

Bindery

❑ deliver flat press sheets ❑ round corner ❑ pad ❑ Wire-O

❑ trim ❑ punch ❑ paste bind ❑ spiral bind

❑ collate or gather ❑ drill ❑ saddle stitch ❑ perfect bind

❑ plastic coat with ❑ score/perforate ❑ side stitch ❑ case bind

❑ fold _____ ❑ plastic comb ❑ tip in

comments _____

Packing ❑ rubber band in #_____ ❑ paper band in #_____

❑ shrink/paper wrap in #_____ ❑ bulk in cartons/maximum weight _____lbs

❑ skid pack ❑ other _____

Shipping ❑ customer pick up ❑ deliver to _____

_____

❑ quote shipping costs separately ❑ send cheapest way ❑ other _____

Miscellaneous instructions _____

12
ORGANIZATIONAL STRATEGIES

How your handbook is organized will also determine how often — and how effectively — it is used. There are a number of simple techniques that you can incorporate into your handbook to make it easier for employees to access the information they need.

a. TABLE OF CONTENTS

Your table of contents should be thorough enough that employees can quickly locate the section they need information on, descriptive enough that they can determine whether the specific information they need will be where they think it is, and concise enough that they don't have to wade through pages and pages of outline to locate a particular topic.

Sample #9 shows an example of a table of contents that is simple, not comprehensive.

b. INDEX

While a table of contents outlines the broad topics included in your handbook, an index goes into greater detail and allows employees to access information based on topic headings or individual subjects.

An index would indicate, for instance, on which pages an employee might find information on time-off benefits or employee leaves.

If your handbook is brief, an index is probably not necessary. If, however, your handbook is extensive, an index can be another means of making the information more readily accessible to employees.

c. INFORMATION AT A GLANCE

Some information is difficult and tedious to explain in normal text. Items where there are several variables and a number of options, in particular, such as benefit information, can be confusing to employees. Charts and tables can be one way to make that information easier to understand and access. The chart shown in Sample #10, for example, presents the necessary information in a readable, understandable format.

d. QUESTION AND ANSWER SECTIONS

What are some of the common questions that employees ask when they begin their tenure with your company? Question and answer sections are a good way of adding variety to your handbook and making it more meaningful to employees. A typical format might follow the style shown in chapter 6, section **a**.

You may find that, once your handbook has been in use for a while, questions crop up from many sources. Some of those questions may be common to many employees. If this is the case, you may want to keep track of the topics most frequently raised and develop a question and answer section in the next edition of your handbook.

e. PHONE LISTINGS

Consider including a telephone guide in your handbook. Again, give careful consideration to how the listing will be used. For example, a simple alphabetical index, by last name, might seem most appropriate.

But what if an employee doesn't know the name of the person they need to contact, only the job duties? Perhaps a second listing would be helpful — one by department, or job classification.

f. MAPS

Finding their way around a new company can be intimidating for employees. Why not make it easier by including maps in your handbook (see Figure #3)?

Similarly, questions on parking may be important to employees. A parking map indicating where — and where not — to park can help (see Figure #4).

g. CONCLUSION

There are many ways that you can make your handbook easy for employees to use — layout and organization are the broad categories that encompass these techniques. Think from a user standpoint as you prepare to go to press with your handbook. If you were a new employee using the handbook for the first time and having a number of questions about the company that you needed answers to, would it be easy to use? Could you find the information you need quickly? Could you get specific answers to your questions — or information on where to go to get those answers?

You are limited only by your imagination and perception. Obviously you'll learn as you go. Be open to input from employees and your handbook committee on how you can make the handbook easier to use. Keep track of these suggestions and incorporate them in revisions.

SAMPLE #9
TABLE OF CONTENTS

CONTENTS

INTRODUCTION
About this handbook	2
About the company	3
Vision, strategies, and values	7

CODE OF CONDUCT
The code	12
Environmental policy	12
Political processes and government relations	13
Conflicts of interest	15
Antitrust laws	17
Your personal commitment	18
Consequences of violating the code	21

SELECTION AND DEVELOPMENT
Hiring	24
Alternative staffing	30
Employee development and training	31

OCCUPATIONAL HEALTH AND SAFETY
Accommodation of employees with disabilities policy	38
AIDS position statement	42
Corporate medical services	42
Drug and alcohol policy	43
Industrial hygiene	50
Safety	51
Smoking	52
Worker's compensation	53

SOCIAL RESOURCE CENTER
Alcohol and drug dependency counseling	56
Pre-retirement counseling	56
Rehabilitation services	57
Work and family programs	57

Other industrial social services   59

EMPLOYEE RELATIONS
"Two-way street" philosophy   62
Employee relations services   63
Peer group resolution   64
Positive discipline policy   69

WORK FORCE DIVERSITY
Corporate commitment to work force diversity   79
Equal employment opportunity policy statement   80
Corporate policy on sexual harassment   83
Policy against harassment   84

EMPLOYEE PROGRAMS AND SERVICES
Anniversary awards   86
Blood donor club   86
BRITE (Being Responsible in Today's Environment)   87
Bus ridership incentive program   87
Energetics club   87
Insurance coverage   88
Loan/rebate program   88
Matching gifts   89
Recreation and leisure   90
Savings bonds   92
Scholarships   92
Shared resources volunteer program   93
Stock purchases   94
Wellness   94

MISCELLANEOUS POLICIES AND INFORMATION
Communications   96
Credit unions   98
Employee files   98
Environmental policy   100
Inclement weather procedures   103
Insider trading policy   104
Life sustaining act award   106

SAMPLE #10
BENEFITS CHART

	Regular benefit (Full time)	**Other benefit (Part time/temporary)**
MEDICAL	Coverage after completing 1 month of service; company provides employee-only coverage. Employee may purchase family coverage.	Coverage after completing 1,000 hours in 12 consecutive months; company proves most of employee-only coverage. Employee may purchase family coverage.
DENTAL	Coverage after completing 1 month of service; company provides employee-only coverage. Employee may purchase family coverage.	Coverage after completing 1,000 hours in 12 consecutive months; company proves employee-only coverage. Employee may purchase family coverage.
LIFE INSURANCE	Coverage after completing 1 month of service; company provides 1-time annual base pay. Employee may purchase supplemental and dependent coverage.	Coverage after completing 1,000 hours in 12 consecutive months; company proves 1 times annuals base pay based on past 12 months. Employee may purchase supplemental and dependent coverage.
VACATION	Eligible after completing 6 months of service; earn: 1-4 years — 10 days; 5-10 years — 15 days; 11-25 years — 1 additional day for each year of service.	Eligible after completing 1,000 hours in 12 consecutive months; earn based on same schedule as regular benefit employee, but accrual prorated based on hours worked.
SICK PAY	Eligible immediately; may take up to 10 days (80 hours) per year.	Eligible after completing 1,000 hours in 12 consecutive months; may take up to 5 days (40 hours) per year.

SAMPLE #10 — Continued

SICK PAY TO CARE FOR ILL CHILD	Must be eligible for sick pay; may take up to 5 days (40 hours) per year. These count as part of the employee's sick days.	Must be eligible for sick pay; may take up to 2½ days (20 hours) per year. These count as part of the employee's sick days.
HOLIDAYS	Eligible immediately for 9 paid holidays (see listing on pp. 3-8).	Eligible after completing 1,000 hours in 12 consecutive months; pay prorated based on hours worked in preceding month.

FIGURE #3
COMPANY MAP

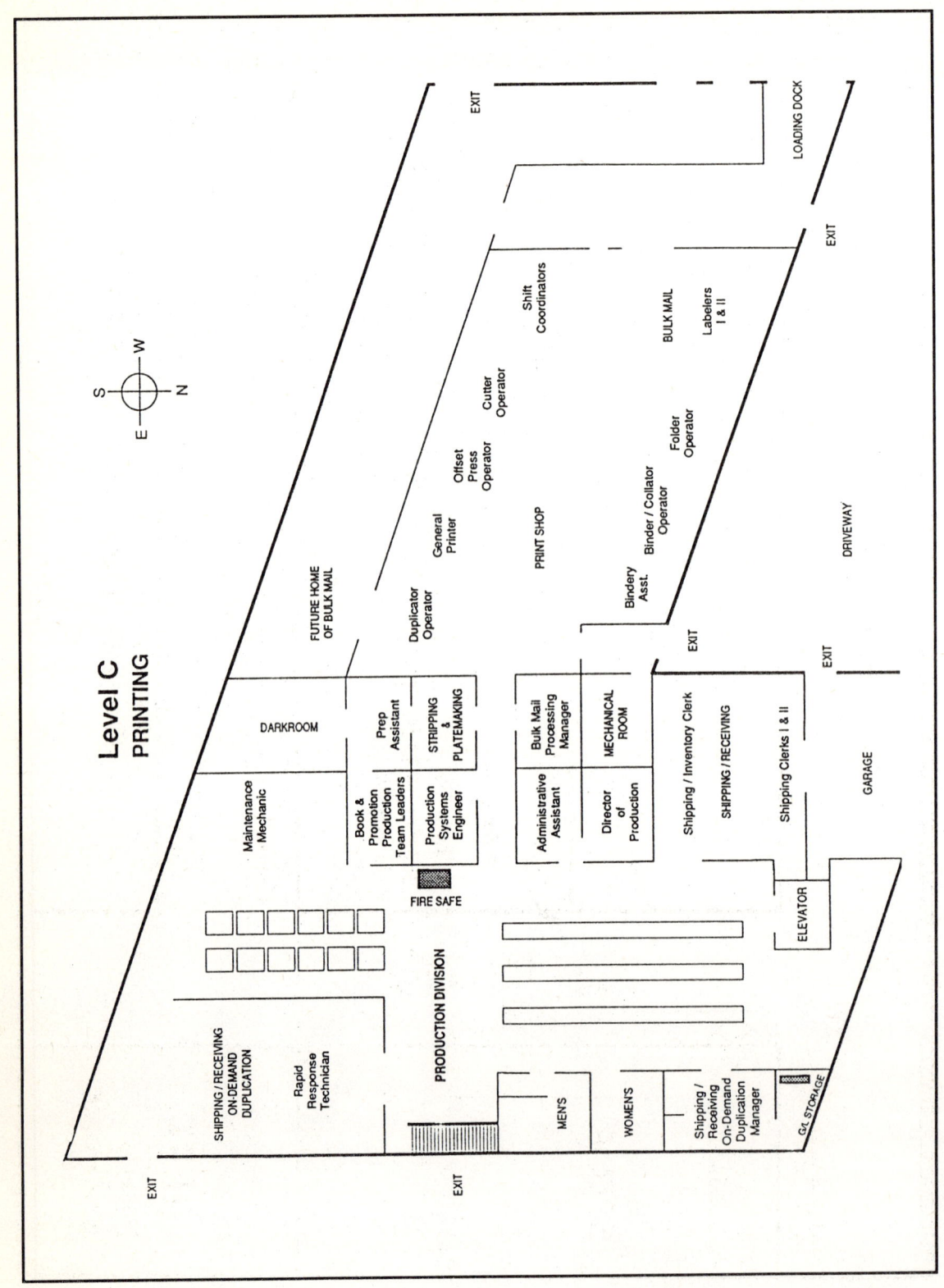

FIGURE #4
PARKING MAP

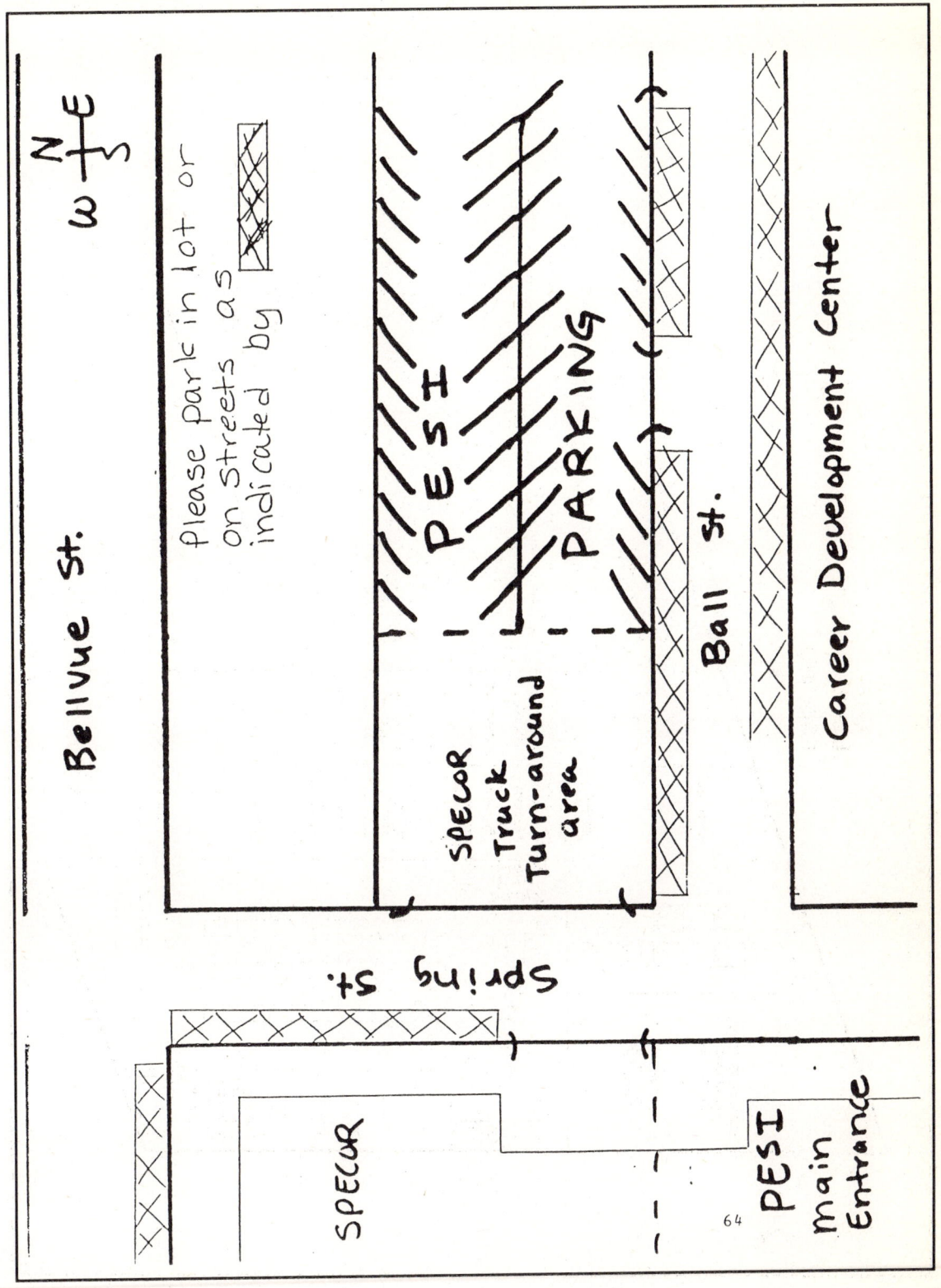

**PART IV
LIVING BY THE BOOK:
HANDBOOK ADMINISTRATION**

13
DON'T STOP NOW...

Whether you decide to produce a handbook that is 200 pages long and perfect-bound, 10 pages long and stapled in the upper left-hand corner, or computerized and accessed through an internal communications network, your job is far from done once the handbook is printed or introduced. Handbook development is not a finite process with a recognizable "end" in sight. Handing out those first drafts is just the beginning.

One of the common problems with personnel handbooks is that they aren't used. Seldom read, they sit on a shelf and gather dust. Revisions are stuffed into the binder, but not looked at. The result is that employees are unaware of the benefits available to them, the sanctions that apply to various aspects of their performance, and the opportunities that exist within their company. A frequent comment is, "I didn't' know that!"

Your best weapon for combating the "I-didn't-know" syndrome is to ensure that employees *do* know — through effective communication. In any company, communication plays a major role both in terms of imparting important information to the work force and in terms of maintaining morale and engendering an atmosphere of teamwork.

What are some common forms of communication that companies have at their disposal? Staff meetings, newsletters, annual reports, bulletin boards — these are just a few examples. Whatever your unique communication tools are, awareness — and organization — are the keys to effectiveness.

Part of the role of the handbook committee is to determine how the handbook will be "communicated" to employees. Communicating your personnel manual involves more than simply handing it out and asking employees to sign a form stating that they're received it. The handbook and its contents should be introduced to employees.

a. MEETINGS

Perhaps the best way to introduce your handbook is in a meeting either with the entire company or by department. At the meeting, each section of the book should be reviewed and employees allowed the opportunity to ask questions or receive clarification on the information. Make overheads of the critical and complex portions of the handbook so they can be reviewed in the meeting.

At this time, you can also provide employees with specific information on how the handbook is to be used and where to go if they need additional information.

When the general meeting is complete, ask your managers and supervisors to continue the discussion in their own staff meetings. Require that supervisors and managers be intimately familiar with the handbook and its contents so they can serve as resources to employees. Both you and your managers should make the handbook a part of ongoing employee communications. Refer to it in staff meetings, one-on-one discussions, etc.

Don't be afraid to talk about the handbook and its contents too much. Repetition is a key to retention. To avoid the "shelf syndrome" with your handbook, make it an integral part of the day-to-day activities of your company and all those in it.

As changes come up or revisions are necessary, call employees back together to discuss those changes. Make sure that they add or delete the appropriate pages and that they understand the implications of any changes made.

b. BULLETIN BOARD

When new handbooks are introduced or as changes are made, make use of your company bulletin boards to post specific items. Consider developing posters that highlight the availability of the handbook or point to critical new bits of information.

c. SUGGESTION BOX

To assure that employees feel that the company handbook is their handbook, invite input. Have a suggestion box or a similar system in place so that employees can contribute their ideas or point out areas that need clarification or modification. Be responsive to the suggestions submitted. One of the failings of many suggestion systems is that managers and company owners don't respond promptly to the suggestions submitted. Get back to employees immediately — whether their ideas will be implemented or not. If you are not going to implement a suggestion, explain why and encourage the employee to continue to submit ideas in the future.

d. TESTING

Consider implementing some form of testing on the contents of the handbook and make it an on-going process — not a one-time activity. Offer an incentive to employees for reading and retaining the information in their handbooks. One company has a quiz it gives to employees after they have received the handbook to show whether they have understood the basics. You might tie performance on such a quiz to some token incentive — movie tickets, gift certificates, etc.

e. MAKING YOUR MANUAL USER FRIENDLY

Here are some additional tips that can you help create a personnel handbook that will be used — and useful.

- Gather handbooks from other companies to generate ideas. How are the books laid out? How is information organized and arranged to aid readability? What makes these various handbooks good or bad? What do you like about these handbooks? What do you dislike?

- Talk to other business owners or personnel managers about the process they went through in putting together their employee handbooks. What did they learn in the process? What tips can they offer you on pitfalls to avoid or suggestions to make your handbook most effective?

- Aim, above all, to increase employee understanding of the operation of your business. Write with the employees' interests in mind. Use a level of writing neither above or below your average reader.

- Establish an on-going handbook committee whose responsibility is to assure that the handbook is kept up to date. The committee might meet on a regular basis to update and modify the handbook, determine when a revision should be issued, and develop ways to best communicate changes to the work force.

- Hold orientation sessions for new employees to go over the handbook and to familiarize them in other ways with the company, its organization and operations.

OTHER TITLES IN THE SELF-COUNSEL BUSINESS SERIES

A SMALL BUSINESS GUIDE TO EMPLOYEE SELECTION
Finding, interviewing, and hiring the right people
by Lin Grensing

This book offers employers practical information on how to successfully select productive employees. It includes sample advertisements, application forms, suggested interview questions, and role-play exercises for the interviewer/applicant exchange. $7.95

Some of the questions answered are:

- What do I need to know before I advertise for the new position?
- How do I screen resumes effectively?
- What questions should I ask the candidates during the interview?
- Do I have to worry about human rights laws when I am hiring?
- What if an employee has AIDS?
- What should I consider before introducing a drug-testing plan at my company?
- What is the best way to make a new employee feel comfortable? How can top employees be encouraged to stay?

MOTIVATING TODAY'S WORK FORCE
When the carrot can't always be cash
by Lin Grensing

In the 1990s, a favorable working environment combined with good worker benefits will eclipse salaries as the prime concern of the work force. Here is a book that tackles the job-satisfaction issue head on. It offers creative options that will help companies increase worker effectiveness. The book shows owners and managers what their employees value most, whether it's a simple pat on the back or an innovative non-monetary reward such as an in-house day-care center or more independence.

Lin Grensing knows the best-kept secrets on how to boost the bottom line by improving productivity through honest praise, promotions, and perks. Her book gives practical applications to various motivational theories and shows how to attain a high level of corporate morale in that all-important work force. $8.95

Contents include:

- Nonmonetary incentives and motivational theory
- How to avoid the motivational fallacies
- How to determine what motivates employees
- Goal setting
- Communication
- Job enrichment
- Flexible benefits

THE FIRST-TIME MANAGER: A SURVIVAL GUIDE
by Theodore Tyssen

If you're going to survive as a manager, you've got to know how to manage people. *People* produce results and managers are judged by what their people accomplish. Productive employees have managers who put people first, because good employees are a company's best resource.

The five-step outlined in the book lets you develop your own people-centered management style and resolve problems before they become blocks to a productive workplace. $7.95

By following each step, you'll know how to —

- Select the right employees for the job
- Provide proper orientation and direction
- Work with your employees to design a productive work environment
- Apply training and skills development when needed
- Provide on-going motivation and support

EFFECTIVE SPEAKING FOR BUSINESS SUCCESS
Making presentations, using audio-visuals, and more
by Jacqueline Dunckel and Elizabeth Parnham

Give dynamic speeches, presentations, and media interviews. When you are called upon to speak in front of your business colleagues, or asked to represent your company in front of the media, do you communicate your thoughts effectively? Or do you become tongue-tied, nervous, and worry about misrepresenting yourself and your business?

Effective communication has always been the key to business success, and this book provides a straightforward approach to developing techniques to improve your on-the-job speaking skills. This book is as easy to pick up and use as a quick reference for a specific problem as it is to read from cover to cover. Whether you want to know how to deal with the media, when to use visual aids in a presentation, or how to prepare for chairing a meeting, this book will answer your questions and help you regain your confidence. $8.95

Contents include:

- Preparing your presentation
- When and where will you speak?
- Let's look at visual aids
- Let's hear what you have to say: rehearsing
- How do you sound?

BUSINESS ETIQUETTE
Make a good impression — gain the competitive edge
by Jacqueline Dunckel

Mind your manners and get ahead! Knowing when to open the door for a colleague or how to accept a gift can sometimes mean the difference between being pigeon-holed in your current position or being offered that attractive promotion. But times have also changed, and the rules once relied on are not always appropriate today. With the growing number of women in company boardrooms and the move toward more international business, a new style of behavior is often called for.

This book is as easy to pick up and use as a quick reference before that special event as it is to read cover to cover. $9.95

Contents include:
- To begin at the beginning — the etiquette of employment
- Department decorum
- Telephone manners
- Meeting manners and boardroom behavior
- Introductions and conversation
- Cultural courtesy
- Table manners
- Eating in and dining out
- Giving and receiving — the etiquette of business gifts
- Manners on the road

GOOD ETHICS, GOOD BUSINESS
Your plan for success
by Jacqueline Dunckel

If you are in business to make a profit — and who isn't — then you need to give thought to the ethics of your business. Ethics doesn't just apply to huge companies with million-dollar accounts; small businesses can benefit from implementing an ethical program too. An ethical approach to business promotes trust: between a business and its customers as well as between employers and employees. That trust creates better employee relations, satisfied customers, and a company respected in the community — which all contribute to greater success — both financial and personal.

This book will help you analyze your own business ethics and those of your employees, colleagues, and suppliers. $8.95

Probe and define your ethics by discussing these topics:
- How to develop a code of ethics
- The importance of leadership
- Owner/management responsibility
- Advertising ethics
- Introducing and maintaining your ethics program
- Measuring your success

THE ENTREPRENEUR'S GUIDE TO GROWING UP
Taking your small company to the next level
by Edna Sheedy

For the owner/manager, growth in his or her small business means working harder and longer and facing new challenges. This is a practical book about organizing, planning, and managing that awkward stage of growth after start-up when the company goes from small to *bigger*. This book speaks clearly about the changes necessary to ensure the passage is a smooth and profitable one. $8.95

Some of the topics covered include:
- Setting your goals
- Growing confidence
- Using your people wisely
- Drawing — or redrawing — your organizational chart
- Hiring management
- Learning how to effectively delegate
- Being an effective leader

Also provided are worksheets and samples to help you plan for your business.

PRODUCING A FIRST-CLASS VIDEO FOR YOUR BUSINESS
Work with professionals or do it yourself
by Dell Dennison, Don Doman, and Margaret Doman

Whether you want to sell and demonstrate your product, build your corporate image, announce new items to the media, train employees, or educate the public about your cause, presenting your message on video may be the answer for you. This book tells you everything you need to know about finding and working with a video production company, or doing it yourself and setting up your own production facility. It offers tips on everything from preparing your employees to appear on camera to making your office look good on video. $14.95

Topics covered include:
- Determining if video is the best way to reach your audience
- Planning your budget and estimating costs
- Finding the right production company
- Writing the script
- Using music, special effects, graphics, and interactive video
- Hiring professional performers or using employees
- Shooting on location or in the studio
- Editing and the postproduction process

KEEPING CUSTOMERS HAPPY
Strategies for success
by Jacqueline Dunckel and Brian Taylor

Customer satisfaction is your company's best asset!

Consumers today demand personal attention from businesses before they spend their money. So, customer service is moving up the priority list in dynamic companies and it is consuming more of their time and budgets; businesses that ignore customer relations do so at their peril.

You need good service to attract customers and keep them coming back, and this book provides plans and programs that have been proven successful by other businesses. No matter what kind of business you are in, this book will help increase profits through improved customer relations. $8.95

Contents include:
- Customer service — what it is and what it is not
- The "why" of customer relations
- The value of service
- Developing a profitable customer relations program
- Setting goals for your business
- Putting your plan together
- Communicating your customer relations program to your employees
- Training employees
- Bringing it all together

PRACTICAL TIME MANAGEMENT
How to get more things done in less time
by Bradley C. McRae

Here is sound advice for anyone who needs to develop practical time management skills. It is designed to help any busy person, from any walk of life, use his or her time more effectively. Not only does it explain how to easily get more things done, it shows you how your self-esteem will improve in doing so. More important, emphasis is placed on maintenance so that you remain in control. Whether you want to find extra time to spend with your family or read the latest bestseller, this book will give you the guidance you need — without taking up a lot of your time! $7.95

Some of the skills you will learn are:
- Learning to monitor where your time goes
- Setting realistic and attainable goals
- Overcoming inertia
- Rewarding yourself
- Planning time with others
- Managing leisure time
- Finding time for physical fitness
- Planning time for hobbies and vacations
- Maintaining the new you

ORDER FORM

All prices are subject to change without notice. Books are available in book, department, and stationery stores. If you cannot buy the book through a store, please use this order form. (Please print)

Name_____
Address_____
_____

Charge to: ❑ Visa   ❑ MasterCard

Account Number_____
Validation Date _____
Expiry Date _____
Signature_____

❑ **Check here for a free catalogue.**

IN CANADA
Please send your order to the nearest location:
Self-Counsel Press
1481 Charlotte Road
North Vancouver, B. C.
V7J 1H1

Self-Counsel Press
8-2283 Argentia Road
Mississauga, Ontario
L5N 5Z2

IN THE U.S.A.
Please send your order to:
Self-Counsel Press Inc.
1704 N. State Street
Bellingham, WA 98225

YES, please send me:
_____ copies of **A Small Business Guide to Employee Selection**, $7.95
_____ copies of **Motivating Today's Work Force**, $8.95
_____ copies of **The First-Time Manager**, $7.95
_____ copies of **Effective Speaking for Business Success**, $8.95
_____ copies of **Business Etiquette**, $9.95
_____ copies of **Good Ethics, Good Business**, $8.95
_____ copies of **The Entrepreneur's Guide to Growing Up**, $8.95
_____ copies of **Producing a First-Class Video For Your Business**, $14.95
_____ copies of **Keeping Customers Happy**, $8.95
_____ copies of **Practical Time Management**, $7.95

Please add $2.50 for postage & handling.
Canadian residents, please add 7% GST to your order.
WA residents, please add 7.8% sales tax.

COMMENTS

Any comments you have on this or any other Self-Counsel publication are welcome. Please use space below.

_____
_____
_____
_____
_____
_____
_____
_____
_____
_____
_____
_____
_____
_____
_____
_____
_____
_____
_____
_____